Brinyild's Journey

Marriage Portrait, 1890s
Andrew and Carrie Erickson, Brinyild's grandparents
Carrie Lynne immigrated from Norway at age 17. Andrew immigrated
from Norway with his father, Tosten, his mother, and six siblings.

Brinyild's Journey

An Iowa Norwegian-American Remembers

by

Horace B. Hegg

Penfield
BOOKS

Acknowledgments

Thanks:

To my wife, Gretchen, who is my best story and who has given her unwavering support for the narrative.

To my children, Philip, Christian, Sara Hegg-Dunne, and Erika Hegg-Arendt, who were interested in these stories but have never seen them in print. I appreciated their enthusiasm as the book progressed.

To the Hudson Public Library staff (Mary, Kathy, Diana, Diane, Erin, and Casey) for their timely problem solving and patience with me as I worked through the computer technicalities and for their interest in the stories.

To my cousin Jerrine (Erickson) Osenga, an environmentalist, for providing important facts about our family history.

To Grinnellian John Ushijima for verifying some essential facts about my visit to Hilo, Hawaii.

To my cousin Lori Erickson-Sessions, a noted writer, for her insightful observations and her encouragement to make a permanent record of the manuscript.

To Erin Kaye Birdsong, poet, clarinetist, student at Yale, and our good friend, who suggested I write my memories of early childhood as a record for my grandchildren. She said, "Go for it!" as I thought about seeking a publisher.

Editors: Joan Liffring-Zug Bourret, Dorothy Crum, Maureen Patterson, and Liz Rolfsmeier.

Cover photography by Joan Liffring-Zug Bourret.

Copyright Horace B. Hegg 2002   ace11172@hotmail.com
ISBN 1-932043-19-5
Library of Congress 2002115233
Published by Penfield Books, 215 Brown Street, Iowa City, Iowa

Dedication

*This narrative is dedicated to the memory
of my Norwegian-American parents, Lester and Palma Hegg,
who lived their lives with grace and dignity
and who bettered the lives of those who knew them.*

*Dr. Lester Hegg and wife, Palma
Wedding portrait, June 16, 1926*

Preface

This narrative is about my life, from memories as a blonde Norwegian-American toddler in the early 1930s to life in the new millennium.

My wife, Gretchen Hegg, and I are from families whose lineage traces back to Norway. Harmony, Minnesota, and Decorah, Iowa, are the hometowns of my parents, Lester and Palma (Erickson) Hegg. Vos, Norway, and Koskomeny, Wisconsin, are represented by fourth-generation Heggs, who settled in Harmony. Hadlund and Oslo, Norway, are represented by the third-generation Ericksons who settled in Burr Oak and Decorah, Iowa.

Leland and Lake Mills, Iowa, are the hometowns of Gretchen's parents, Gilbert Thompson and Clara (Charlson) Thompson. Ancestors of Gilbert Thompson came from Vang, Valdres, and Gudbransdal, Norway, to Calmar, Iowa. Ancestors of Clara (Charlson) Thompson came from Stavanger and Lake Mjosen, Norway, to Mt. Horeb, Wisconsin, and moved on to Leland, Illinois.

Our Norwegian-American families retained the culture of our ancestors. Lefse and lutefisk were prominent fare during the Christmas season in the Hegg home in Rock Valley, Iowa. A big package of homemade lefse would find its way to our door each year, a gift from a Norwegian patient of my father, Dr. Lester Hegg. The table prayer is still given in Norwegian on special occasions. The smorgasbord dinners at the Lutheran church in neighboring Hudson, South Dakota, were occasions to be remembered; Leland and Lake Mills had similar celebrations. Leland High School even incorporated the two food staples into the high school cheer.

"Lutefisk, Lefse, *Tus Ku Te Ha,* Leland High School, Rah! Rah! Rah!"

This narrative may find the Norwegian mystique in a subdued stance, although it is surely there in the substrata. I hope you enjoy!

— *Horace B. Hegg*

Contents

Part 1
Gaining a Foothold

Part 2
Stepping Stones

Part 3
Measured Steps

Part 4
Footprints

A 1904 view of the homestead of Tosten Erickson, who immigrated in 1870. He brought his wife, Karen, and seven children from Norway to Burr Oak, Iowa. He was the great-grandfather of Horace Brinyild Hegg.

Part 1

Gaining a Foothold

Horace Brinyild Hegg, 1931
Two years old, Decorah, Iowa

Upper Iowa River near Decorah, Iowa

Grandpa Erickson's home, Decorah, Iowa

The Beginning: Decorah, Iowa

I was born in Decorah, Iowa, on February 1, 1929. My mother, Palma, and I lived with her parents, Andrew and Carrie Erickson, while my father attended medical school in Chicago. I remember one evening when Mother and I were returning from a trip to the grocery store. She said, "Your daddy is here." I looked at my father, Lester, as we came into the kitchen. "Go over to your daddy." I went to this shy stranger who set me on his lap. This is my first recollection of my father. It was at least two years more before I would have him in my young life.

Lester Hegg and son Horace when Lester was in medical school in Chicago.

Andrew and Carrie had moved from a farm near Burr Oak, Iowa, to Decorah, twelve miles south. Their house was two stories and had a large porch with wide steps that led to the back-yard. A huge cottonwood tree stood by the barn at one corner of the lot. Lilies of the valley grew alongside the walk that led from the porch steps to the street sidewalk. Two red pines and a Whit-ney crabapple tree completed the backyard scene. The house is standing today at the corner of Leif Erickson Drive and Center Street. Luther College is just a few blocks to the west on the drive.

Grandpa Andrew often took me for walks and would read to me from *National Geographic*. He once took me to a carnival in town, where I rode the merry-go-round and was scared to look to the middle for fear I would fall into a black hole.

An ongoing concern of the family was the idea that Otto, one of Palma's brothers who was also living at home, was being taken advantage of by his boss at Hutchinson's grocery store, where the pay was low and there was no chance for advancement. This didn't cramp his style. He was a dresser who might show up at a family picnic wearing a white suit and tie with a boiled collar and white shoes to match. If Otto had to choose between bettering himself and going dancing on Saturday night, my guess is that he would have chosen the dancing. He later went to California, married a charming lady, and worked in a store to a happy end.

Palma's youngest brother, Paul Sherman, was also living at home while attending Luther College. During the summer, he drove an ice truck and would deliver a big chunk of ice to the icebox, which was usually located in the kitchen. Mother worried that the work was too difficult for him, that the ice was too heavy. I was to stay out of his bedroom while he was sleeping. These were good times. He once took me sledding on the frozen Upper Iowa River. He also took me to a football game between Luther and Gustavus Adolphus. Luther lost the game, but I got to eat a Hershey candy bar.

Palma and Sherman went to the dance pavilion north of Decorah one evening, and I didn't like it one bit. I took it out on grandpa after they had gone, and he had to change my diaper. He placed me in a washtub and filled it with water up to my waist. However, the evening didn't turn out so bad. I slept in Grandpa's and Grandma's bed, and in the middle of the night I was awakened by a loud noise. When I asked what it was, Grandpa said it was "roompa," which meant "the bear."

Grandpa died in December of 1931. My mother came out of his room off the kitchen and said, "He's gone." The funeral was right in the house. I remember sliding down the banister leading into the hallway during the visitation.

My mother was born March 19, 1903, on the family farm near Burr Oak, Iowa. She had eight brothers: Carl farmed near Bear Creek east of Burr Oak; Leif moved to Canada to work for Robin Hood Mills in Saskatoon; William farmed the family farm and served with the American Expeditionary Forces in France during the first World War; Albert farmed two miles down the road from the home place; Fritjof died at age eleven, a victim of an influenza epidemic; Silas became the general manager of an International Truck division in Madison, Wisconsin; Otto eventually worked for a grocery chain in California; and Sherman became an owner of a Dodge-Plymouth dealership in Cedar Falls, Iowa.

My mother attended country school through the eighth grade. She then enrolled at Upper Iowa University to study music and attend classes.

Palma, age sixteen
Decorah High School

Decorah High School days
Palma, top

When it was discovered that she had not attended high school, Palma was sent back to Decorah, where she roomed in town. She attended high school classes during the week and spent weekends at the farm. She graduated in May 1921 and enrolled that summer in a normal teacher-training course at Iowa State Teachers College in Cedar Falls. She then taught country school near Burr Oak, where she had Uncle Albert's daughter Shirley as a student.

Country school class picnic, Palma Erickson, teacher, Burr Oak, Iowa

My father, Lester, was born November 4, 1897, in Harmony, Minnesota. He had an older brother, Clarence, and a younger brother, Oral. Lester had to leave school at age thirteen to tend to the family farm after his father died suddenly of a heart attack. His mother, Oliva, was known for her home remedies for the sick and administered many to her neighbors during the 1917 flu epidemic. Lester was also working several farms during the epidemic even though he was ill from bronchitis. Somewhere during this time, he resolved to become a medical doctor. He confessed this to a neighbor friend one day as they were resting in the shade of a hay wagon. The neighbor told me many years later that when he asked Lester why he thought he could become a doctor, Lester said it was because, "He had a hard heart."

My mother called my father "Les." Her brother, "Si," introduced Lester to Palma. According to all reports, it was love at first sight. Les was attending Luther College at the time and had to walk by the home place on his way to classes. At one time, I visualized a chance meeting at the corner of Leif Erickson Drive and First Street. A picture of them together at the farm eliminated that possibility.

The Andrew Erickson family, 1926
Back row, L. to R.: William Axel, Silas Victor Norman, Carl Torvall,
Otto Lee, Leif Ferdinand, Albert Calmar. Front row, L. to R: Palma Elizabeth,
Father Andrew, Mother Carrie, Paul Sherman

Back to School

*Lester and Palma Hegg on their wedding day
at the Little Brown Church, Nashua, Iowa, June 16, 1926*

Lester borrowed ten thousand dollars from an aunt, entered prep school at Luther College, and seven years later graduated cum laude from the college at age twenty-eight. He worked at a variety of jobs during the times he was not in school. While an undergraduate at Luther College, he often went the whole day having eaten only a bowl of oatmeal with raisins and milk for his breakfast. He sold carpeting. He sold life insurance for Iowa Life and was offered a district agency if he were to continue with them.

Lester and Palma were married June 16, 1926, at the nationally known Little Brown Church in Nashua, Iowa. Lester was a true romantic. I remember hearing him hum the tune "Little Brown Church in the Vale" on many occasions.

After graduation from Luther College and his marriage to Palma, he enrolled in the two-year medical school in Grand Forks, North Dakota. An aunt lived there, and it was the cheapest school he could find at the

The Hegg farm, where Dr. Lester Hegg was raised, near Harmony, Minnesota

time. Anna Bales had married Harry, an Englishman who was well off, and they lent Lester money to continue his schooling.

Palma and Lester lived in Grand Forks during his two years at the medical school. He worked at a funeral parlor while attending classes. After graduation, Lester enrolled at Rush Medical School, which later became part of the University of Chicago. Here, he managed the medical fraternity house for his room and board.

After graduating from Rush, Lester interned at the university hospital in Iowa City. He once said that he saw more unusual cases at Cook County Hospital in Chicago in a week than he saw during the whole year in Iowa City. Lester was on duty one day during his internship when a little girl was admitted in a diabetic coma. He treated her using the latest procedure with positive results but received criticism from his resident physician for not calling him in on the case. A week later a young man was admitted in a diabetic coma. The resident physician handled this case using an outdated procedure and the patient did not survive. At the next staff meeting, Dr. Hegg called the offending doctor on the carpet for using the outdated procedure.

Dr. Hegg took a job with the Department of the Interior, Indian Affairs Bureau, to earn enough money to open his own practice. He worked at the Rosebud Reservation in Pine Ridge, South Dakota. After six months, he returned to Decorah to take us to Beresford, South Dakota, where he intended to set up a practice.

Go West, Young Family

My only recollection of Beresford, South Dakota, is waking up in the rear seat of the car one Sunday, climbing out onto the street and up onto a high curb. My parents were in a restaurant and had to come out to claim the lost boy.

It was not easy starting a practice in those days, so when news came that a doctor had passed away in Rock Valley, Iowa, we were soon on our way there for Dad to begin a new practice. I can remember the ride to the new home. We took a big Buick coupe, which I don't remember ever seeing again.

Rock Valley was a typical western Iowa town laid out in a grid with the streets running compass north and the business district at the center. It was founded in 1879 and may have originally been named "Irene." (A railroad survey map of Iowa (1877) shows that name at the Rock Valley site.) There is a town in South Dakota named Irene, and it could be presumed that someone took the name with them when they moved. At any rate, the town's most distinguishing character is its wide streets. On a three-block stretch of the business district, diagonal parking at both curbs with double-diagonal parking in the middle of the street was the norm. On Wednesday and Saturday nights, the farmers would fill all the spaces as they did their shopping.

The businesses in Rock Valley included four grocery stores, two drugstores, a bakery, three hardware stores, a barbershop, a dry goods store, a bank, two meat markets, a shoe shop, a hotel, three restaurants, a movie theater, a variety store, a dentist, two doctors, a candy distributor, two furniture stores, eleven churches, two law firms, and the train depot.

The Milwaukee Road passenger train arrived from Milwaukee at nine o'clock in the morning and from Sioux Falls at five o'clock in the afternoon. Although I was not to hang around downtown, it was all right to go down to the station to watch the "five o'clock" come into the depot. My friends and I would watch for the steam engine to round the bend a mile west of town. There could be several passenger cars, and we would dutifully wave at passengers who were looking out the windows, and they often would wave back.

In 1933, the population was about sixteen hundred. Nearly half the people were of Dutch extraction with the remainder a mixture of Irish, German, and a few Norwegians. Lester had three years each of the German, Greek, and Latin languages while a student at Luther and was to learn Dutch as well. Many of the elderly from Holland were more at home with their native language.

Dick and Hetz Roeloff ran one of the grocery stores. In those days, when the customer came in with a list, either one of the two would fill the order. They also had a delivery truck and would bring your order right to your kitchen. Often a small bag of peppermints was included. They enjoyed their work and smiled and laughed with each customer—making it a social occasion.

Foppe's Pioneer Store had a complete line of dry goods, in addition to a grocery department. A central office serviced all departments. The clerks in individual departments placed the money in a small cylinder container and it was transported by air pressure through a tube to the central office. Euda Bernard would send the change and sales slip back to the appropriate department by this system. Four sisters headed the women's departments and were too busy to ever have married.

Roelof's grocery store, one of at least four in Rock Valley, 1940s

Getting Started in Rock Valley

Our first home, after arriving in Rock Valley, was a rooming house owned by Fred Relander. It was located across the street from the Catholic church and two blocks east of the main downtown intersection. Lester rented a couple of rooms for office space over one of the hardware stores on Main Street.

In 1933, there was no Chamber of Commerce to welcome a new business to the town. The residing doctor had his own stable of patients and was not looking for competition. He dispensed his own prescriptions and seemed capable of treating both two-legged and four-legged patients with equal ease. The town's two-story frame hospital was closed and in a state of disrepair—perhaps a testament to some unfortunate medical practices of the past.

Many days went by without a single patient as Dr. Hegg waited to provide his services. One day there was some commotion on Main Street. A man had rolled his car over on a country road, receiving a gash to his head that literally left his scalp dangling. They carried the fellow up the stairs to the office. Dr. Hegg sent him on his way after some careful cleaning of the wound and over one hundred stitches. His walking around the town the next few days was the best advertising Dr. Hegg could ask for.

Once people started coming in, Dr. Hegg was able to make some long-range plans. He went to one of the drugstores and suggested they modernize their inventory of drugs. If so, he would send all his prescriptions to them. Arrangements with the bank allowed construction of a small brick office building next to a ladies' hat shop on the north end of Main Street.

The Hegg family moved to an upstairs apartment in a house with a grand staircase. Harvey Bernard, a pharmacist at the Corner Drugstore, and his wife, Euda, owned the house and lived in the downstairs. There was a living room, kitchen, bath, and bedroom. Each night Palma would make up my bed on the leather-covered horsehair sofa in the living room. She would push a couple of chairs against the sofa so I wouldn't fall out of the "bed."

The Early Years

Those early years at Harvey and Euda's house were important ones for me. Several future schoolmates lived within a few blocks. Hale Pember, Eugene Vanderwell, Ray Schutz, Bob Potts, and Tom McGill were to form a part of the graduating class of 1946. There was a beehive of activity in the neighborhood with few restraints on our activities.

Mae Bergsma was the matriarch of the neighborhood, and we seemed to congregate at her back door. She baked bread every day and, if we dropped by, she would supply us with buttermilk pop and a peanut butter and jam sandwich. Mae's youngest boy, Earl, who was in high school, was our instructor in making skis from barrel staves, rubber guns from old inner tubes, and homemade kites. Because all of the houses had wooden shingles back then, we would carve arrows out of old shingles. They were launched into the air using a long stick with a string attached.

Mae had a niece who would visit her from the neighboring town of Hull. Bernice Meylink married Maynard Newhouse, who farmed near Burr Oak. They were neighbors of Bill and Hilda Erickson, who bought his parents' farm when Grandpa and Grandma Erickson moved to Decorah. Years later, Bernice and Maynard bought the farm from Aunt Hilda and they have lived on it to the present day.

Mae would call me Brinyild, which is my Norwegian middle name. The name came from my great-great uncle Brinyild Hegg, whose gravestone is in the Harmony, Minnesota, cemetery.

She developed cancer and, as the illness progressed, was bedridden. One day, she asked for me to visit her. I remember the sadness I felt knowing that she would soon be gone. I don't know what things we talked about, but there were no tears shed. She was the only one in my early days who called me Brinyild and that made it special for me.

John Corwin moved away after only two years, but I have to include him in the group. We would walk home from first grade at noon and often got into a fight over something. Then we would walk back to school together. John had the benefit of an older brother to pick on so I usually came out on the short end of any physical confrontation with him. I bragged that I ate Wheaties for breakfast, but John ate oatmeal and that seemed to have more power. I can remember taking money out of

Rock Valley, 1930s

Mother's purse one day and giving it to John as some kind of buy off. It was about a dollar and thirty-six cents, which was probably a week's grocery money. Fortunately, his mom called Mother to ask if she was missing any change.

Dad once asked John how I was doing in first grade. John told my dad I was always "looking at his coloring." Another commandment broken, so I was not too sorry to see John move out of town. My folks let me visit him at Luverne, Minnesota. John's grandmother, Lottie, was my chauffeur for the trip. She was eighty at the time and had run over a couple of curbs in her recent driving history, but we arrived without incident.

The Corwins had bought a farm on the outskirts of Luverne where they raised sheep. John and I went to one of the fields and hit golf balls with wooden shafted clubs. When he would come to visit me, Dad would see that we put on the boxing gloves! John moved to Sioux City, and I lost track of him.

One day we heard that gypsies were camped in a large meadow near Fairview, South Dakota, just seven miles west of town. Mother and I hitched a ride to see the campsite with Richard Kearns from Foppe's Pioneer Store. Horses and wagons were scattered about, and the gypsies were busy with their chores. As we sat in the auto, two young gypsy girls approached and suddenly threw open the back door, grabbed me by the leg, and started pulling me out. Mother grabbed my arm and shouted for them to go away. The girls went away laughing as they "counted coup" for the day.

Dad bought me a bicycle after I finished first grade. It was the second balloon tire bike in town—an American Eagle from the Gamble store. Soon after, my chums had their bikes, too. We would race each other around the block. Since my bike had 25-inch wheels as opposed to the 26-inch wheels on my friends' bikes, I would always get a lead until the halfway mark. I found that I had to leave the street for the sidewalk to have a fair shot at winning the race. Unfortunately, on one occasion, an older lady in a big black overcoat was walking in the same direction as I was racing. I tooted my horn at her, but at the last minute, she crossed over to my passing side. It was she or the big cottonwood; I took the coward's way out. We went down in a heap, and she rolled over and looked at me, all the while cussing me in Dutch. The only word I recognized was the local constable's name. A proclamation the next day made it illegal to ride on the sidewalks! I got all the credit for that bit of legislation.

At Christmastime the city would decorate a big tree at the main intersection in downtown Rock Valley. The Valley State Bank placed a Three Wise Men scene on their roof. The Saturday before Christmas, Santa would show up riding in the back of the town dray, tossing sacks of candy to all the children. One year I had the chicken pox and was surprised when Santa came into the apartment with a sack for me. I looked in the back closet later that same day and discovered a cowboy hat and some wooly chaps that were to be found under the tree. It was about that time that Santa lost some of his credibility.

Father Knows All

Dad claimed he knew about everything that I did. This was hard for me to believe even as a five-year-old. One day I got up from the table and went into the bathroom and shouted, "What am I doing now?" The answer came back from the kitchen, "You're standing in front of the mirror looking at yourself." Of course, he was right!

It wasn't until many years later that I found out that my every move was reported to Dr. Hegg. One time several of us were intent upon sampling apples from Mrs. T's orchard; it was dusk going on twilight when she came out the door. We all ran with me leading the pack. I heard a voice say, "I see you, son of Doc Hegg." Dad never let on, but he knew.

There were times when it was good that folks were watching out for me. One day I came to the schoolhouse playground. Two sisters were swinging on the rings. Since I was too short to reach the rings from the ground, I had to get up on the platform. Finally I asked the older sister if I could swing. She flipped the ring at me, and it hit me square on the forehead. I chased her for three blocks, but couldn't catch her so I marched back to the rings with a big bump on my forehead. On the steps of the platform, with my hands on my hips, I issued my ultimatum to the younger sister who was on the same ring, "If you don't let me swing, I'll chase you home, too." She let that ring fly, and it hit me right on the bump on my forehead. This time blood was flowing down my face as I chased her the same route as her sister. One of the neighbor ladies rushed out as though she was expecting me. Dad sewed me up and he asked, "How did this happen again?" He just laughed.

Driving the Car

As I grew older, I realized my Dad was not a very good driver. He would start the car on a cold winter morning, race the engine and then put it in low gear, race the engine some more and go. Shifting gears was always a battle. There was no speed limit, and it soon got around that Dr. Hegg would drive well over sixty mph. There was an S-curve two miles west of Hull on Highway 18 that was poorly banked by today's standards. He would barrel through that curve without easing off the gas pedal.

U.S. Highway 18 was paved to Rock Valley but was gravel from there to the South Dakota line. A new bridge was being constructed across the Rock River west of town. We took a ride out to see it one Sunday afternoon, and after having a look at the bridge construction, Dad realized he would have to drive the car in reverse several blocks to get turned around. That was not acceptable to him, so he decided to drive down the embankment to a temporary construction road that would get us out of there. Mother and I got out of the car—fully expecting it to go head over heels down the embankment. The dust settled, and we slid down to the waiting car and headed for home. He never would have made it in reverse.

There was a Ford dealer and a Dodge garage. Dad bought his cars from the Ford dealer and had his service work done there. One day he drove a few blocks from the garage and the engine melted for lack of oil. Dad paid for a new engine, because he knew that the young mechanic who forgot to replace the oil probably would be fired if the dealer had to cover the cost. The mechanic bought the business several years later.

When the war came along the rule was that no one should own more than two cars. A doctor in Sioux City had to sell a 1941 Lincoln with twelve thousand miles on the odometer. He wanted sixteen hundred dollars for it; Dad offered him thirteen hundred and won the flip. A year went by before he noticed that the tires had been recapped.

The Lincoln was blue; it had sixteen-inch wheels and was freewheeling, which meant that when one let up on the gas, the transmission would disengage from the engine. The effect of this was that one had to be constantly working the brakes to keep from running up the backside of any car directly in front. It also had turn signals and push-button doors on the inside, which was high tech in those days. Pull-out refrigerator-type handles on the outside were another feature.

One day, Dr. Hegg drove an expectant mother and her husband to the hospital in LeMars for delivery of the baby. The husband was so excited that when he tried to open the door of the car, he turned the handle down and right off. There was no handle on the right side for the rest of the time that we owned the car. Replacement parts were not available because of the war, but it was all right because the door could still be opened from the inside.

Dr. Hegg was a fearless driver. One year, the river had flooded, and the road west of town was under water. Dad asked Ted Bauman, the Standard Oil station owner, if he would ride along on an emergency call. They got through the half-mile of flooded road, but both were dizzy watching the water swirling by the car. Once, Dad came over a hill on a country road and hit a big hog. The front of the 1941 Ford caved in, and the hog flew at least a hundred feet in the air.

Dr. Hegg often had patients at Sacred Heart Hospital in Le Mars. He would leave for his hospital rounds very early in order to cover the sixty-mile round trip and be in the office by 8 o'clock. One morning, on his way to the hospital, a rooster pheasant flew through the windshield, striking Dad on the forehead. He drove the rest of the way, about twenty-six miles, to the hospital. The nuns were amazed that this accident victim was able to drive at all. The doctors said Dad's felt hat that was pulled down over his eyes saved him from serious injury.

Fireworks were still legal in Iowa in the early thirties. All my friends had some assortment including cherry bombs, roman candles, one-inchers, skyrockets, worms, and sparklers. It was fun to put firecrackers under tin cans to see how high they would blow. This led to a serious mishap, however. Carol, a niece of Harvey and Euda, watched me place a small firecracker under mother's lawn chair. Unfortunately, Carol was holding a lighted one-incher in her hand. The rest of the day was pretty much shot, with Dad ministering to her eyes. I never had the courage to ask Carol if her vision was permanently impaired from this incident.

The New House

Mother and Dad made plans to buy a lot and build a house. The 150' by 150' lot was on the southeast corner of the block on the east edge of town. Corny and Ada Rozeboom sold the lot off the end of their pasture, so we had cows and chickens grazing to the west of us as well as pasture across the street to the east.

My parents chose a typical one-and-a-half story Cape Cod-style design. A single garage was built separate from the house at one corner of the lot. The front walk extended to the end of the lot line, and then there was a grass lane about 200 yards long, adjacent to the pasture, leading to Corny and Ada's lot line. The lane was shaded on both sides by elm trees, and it was fun to run the path on your bicycle and fly up the little bump where our sidewalk began.

The downstairs of the house had a 26-foot-long living room with a fireplace. There was also a dinette, kitchen, a half bath, a dining room, the foyer, and stairway directly to the second floor, which had a master bedroom on the left and a bedroom and bath on the right. The basement was dug using a team of horses and a dragline; the foundation was concrete block. The siding was 10-inch clapboard; there were two dormers at the front, and green shutters, which really worked, framed the windows. We moved into this new home in the spring of 1936.

We were anticipating the arrival of a new member of the family in late summer. I was excited about the prospect of having a little baby to push around the living room in the crib that was assembled there. The new hardwood floors and lack of furniture in the room made this seem like a fun thing for the baby and me. Finally, on a hot summer evening Mother said, "It's time to go."

The new house, 1936

Forever Changed

Horace and Peer, summer 1938

On August 26, l936, a 10-pound, 14-ounce baby brother came into the world. His name was Peer Siegfried Hegg, and our world would be forever changed. He was a beautiful baby, and I wanted to push him around the living room in his crib. However, after taking a look at him, I decided he was too small for that.

Peer grew up very fast. He was always bigger than his age by at least a year—and maybe two. Dad wouldn't take him off the place during his first two years. I think it was because of the polio epidemic and other communicable diseases. Dad bought him a chain-drive tricycle the summer he turned four. He would take off down the sidewalk toward town while I shouted for him to come back. I couldn't catch him by running after him.

He was a jolly kid and could get us all laughing. One of his expressions, when introduced to an adult, was "Hi, Stinky." I can remember this happening when we visited Uncle Sherman in Dubuque. Peer and I rode downtown with "Sherm." We were introduced to a lot of people, and whenever we met someone new, he chirped this greeting. It always got a laugh.

A Lot to Learn
About a Lot of Things

My formal schooling began when I was five years old. I attended first grade in a two-room frame building with a hallway located directly behind the three-story brick elementary and high school building. The two teachers were in complete command of their teaching environment. Miss Lammers, the first grade teacher, was not one to show much emotion. Helen McNamara, the second grade teacher, had a nice laugh and was one of those people who made a difference in how one viewed the learning experience.

There is one altercation that sticks out in my memory. A student had made some sort of transgression that called for discipline. He was ordered into the hallway and the first grade teacher was summoned. Buckle overshoes were beneath the coat racks, and we could hear those overshoes flying about and loud shouting. No one got out of his seat nor did we ask any questions when the teacher and young man returned. The matter never got beyond the doors of the building. I never did learn what the ruckus was about, but it did leave an impression.

The little frame building didn't amount to much. There was no drinking fountain or rest room so one had to go to the big building next door for those. The building was sold that summer, moved off the property, and made into two small homes on lots near our house. A huge slide replaced the building. The slide became a favorite place to play tag. We would climb over the safety rail and slide down the poles as an escape route from whoever was "it." We would also sit on snow blocks to ride the slide and would almost be airborne by the time we reached the bottom.

I learned about taking care of lawns. Dad hired Louie to mow and weed the yard once a week. Louie was unemployed so the three dollars he made was important for putting some food on the table for his family. One day, Dad set me to work pulling weeds from an area between the curb and sidewalk with orders that the weeds had to come out roots and all or they would grow back. When I got through there was not a weed in sight nor was there any grass—just dirt.

As I grew older I took over the lawn-mowing chores. This meant pushing a reel mower, catching the grass, bagging it up, and carrying it to the curb. At the end of the day there would be a substantial pile of fresh-cut grass. Leo Grosenberg would come by in his pickup truck, and I would help him load the grass into the truck to feed to the two Belgian stud horses he kept in his corral just down the street. Harvey, a big fiery roan, and Prince, a big, gentle black, loved the fresh grass. Leo would give me a dime for making the feed available. One could buy a double-dip ice cream cone at the bakery for a dime, so it was a good deal for me.

One day when Leo came to pick up the grass, a kid named Eddie happened along. When it came time for the payment, Leo handed me the dime saying, "You two can split it." Now if he had given me two nickels, there wouldn't have been a problem. I mumbled to Eddie that I didn't have any change and that I would get back to him. Eddie was not a close friend; in fact, I hardly knew him. He lived on the west end of town and went to parochial school. Weeks would pass before I would see Eddie again. He would mention something about the nickel, and I would have no change. Years later he would look at me, and I would grin weakly but still no nickel.

From the book *Rock Valley Records and Recollections*

Second Grade
Teacher, Miss McNamara, center, second row; back row, "Brinyild," right of teacher

– 29 –

Another Norwegian

One day the band director came to our house. I had just begun the fourth grade and Harley Christopherson was busy recruiting new members for the high school orchestra. He was a full-blooded Norwegian, so his opinion carried quite a bit of weight in the Hegg household. He thought I was ready to begin playing an instrument, and after examining my teeth and bite, he decided that the clarinet would be just the thing for me. A new clarinet soon arrived and it was a beauty—steel—and could be assembled from four pieces. The bell was gold so I presumed a golden tone would come forth. It was a King and cost one hundred dollars, which was a lot of money for a clarinet in those days. I was soon sitting in the back row in the clarinet section of the orchestra with "Pudd" VandeVelde, who was in sixth grade. This was on-the-job training, and I was excited to be in the company of older students.

From the book *Rock Valley Records and Recollections*

The Rock Valley High School Band
Horace with his steel clarinet, second row, third from left;
Harley Christopherson, wearing tie, second from right

Harley Christopherson was a confessed hypochondriac. One night after we had gone to bed, we heard the sound of someone running up the stairs. It was Harley in the midst of a grand panic attack; he had to have the doctor's assurance that he wasn't dying.

Harley was a violinist, so he was able to put together a good string section, but didn't offer much help with the clarinet. A couple of years went by before I realized that the upper lip should not be in the way of the upper teeth and the mouthpiece!

During the summer I played in the town band. We practiced on Monday night and played in the town square on Wednesday night. A portable grandstand was hauled in, and cars were allowed to park all around. After each number, listeners would toot their car horns, and the band would play some more. The stand had lights all around, and there were bugs everywhere, but the band played on. At the end of the summer, members each received two dollars and fifty cents, courtesy of the City Council.

Early in the summer, Harley developed a stomachache that resulted in his having his appendix removed. The other doctor did the surgery, and it seemed that all Harley talked about, in the next couple of band rehearsals, was what a wonderful job he had done. It was pretty galling for me to sit and listen to that.

The doctor-patient relationship had no middleman in Rock Valley. Office hours started at 8:00 A.M. six days a week. You came in and waited your turn. No nurse, no secretary, just the cleaning lady. It seemed to work. Our house phone rang simultaneously with the office phone, so mother could operate as the message center. When she was out, Ann VerWye, the telephone operator, would take messages. Ann was a big help to the practice since she knew all the sick folks in town, and a couple of phone calls would usually locate Dr. Hegg. I believe she slept by the switchboard.

That same summer I fell in with some kids in my neighborhood who were new to the town. It was green apple season, and we knew where an unguarded tree was waiting. The tree was part of a garden plot just off the edge of town. Getting the apples wasn't enough for my friends. The next thing I knew, one of them was running down the rows of sweet corn. Then the rows of beans got it, and some cabbages went flying. I stood by during this carnage, weakly submitting that we shouldn't be doing this.

Baseball 1940
Horace, left, and his "Support Group:" Tom, Ray, Bill, Robert, Bob, Eugene

When the enormity of the situation hit us, we sneaked away like the vandals that we were.

The next morning at about half past six, there was a knock on the door. I looked out the bedroom window and there was the constable's pickup truck. Dad came up the stairs, and I confessed that I had been at the garden. He drove over to have a look, and when he came back, without a word, brought out the belt. "Do you have any money?" he asked. I responded, "Two dollars and fifty cents." We drove down to the gas station, where the owner of the garden had his business. I handed over the money, sobbing an apology. The kind old man said, "I'll buy some poor kid a pair of shoes with this."

My "friends" never got a call from the constable, and one of them probably got a new pair of shoes. I was confined to the yard for the next two weeks, and by then the summer was over. My "friends" had disappeared, and the rumor was that they had moved to Sioux City.

Baseball Is Big

Baseball was the major sport interest in Rock Valley. A Work Progress Administration project allowed for the construction of a ballpark with lights and a concrete stadium large enough to seat 1,900 fans. There was room for equipment storage, locker space, and shower facilities under the seating area. Two concrete dugouts were provided for the teams, and high wooden fences surrounded the park.

A genuine semi-pro team brought reputable ball players to play on Tuesday evenings during the summer. Folks could park their cars inside the park around the outfield and sit in them to watch the game. A concession stand sold popcorn, hot dogs, and ice cream. The firemen, who were in charge of the games, hired a manager who handled the players and scheduled the visiting teams. Kids spent most of the game outside the stadium hawking foul balls, which were worth ten cents when redeemed at the gate. I remember the battery of Roy Jones and Joe Blair, who were impeccable in their demeanor. They were masters at their positions and could be counted on to keep the team in any game. Blair took a foul tip right in the throat one night. He shook it off and continued to play.

Our favorite player was Kenny Glaze, who played second base. He could field like a big leaguer, and you could tell he loved to play. He lived in town during the season and was hired to instruct baseball to the youth. During the summer, twenty of us practiced every morning. We did batting and fielding drills, then divided into two groups to play a game. I remember one bit of advice from the baseball summer camp: Baseball shoes should be one- and one-half size smaller than your street shoes. We idolized Kenny; to us he was like Phil Rizzuto of the New York Yankees. After the war, he became the recreation director at Aberdeen, South Dakota.

The semi-pro team seldom played away from home; their opponents were often road teams traveling through the Midwest. Towns within sixty miles who had night baseball games were interested in playing against our team when they could be scheduled.

There were many traveling teams in the thirties. The House of David was the most memorable. This was a religious cult, and the players turned over all their worldly goods to join. They didn't believe in shaving so all the players had long hair and long beards. They were noted for their dexterity with the baseball and performed "pepper games" as part of their warm-up routine. This consisted of four or five players facing a batter from about fifteen paces. One would field the batted ball, and then the ball would pass from one player to the next so that you could hardly follow what was happening. It was a great show, and the players knew how to entertain. They traveled all over the country and played year-round.

During one baseball game, I got myself into a tough situation. I was standing at the top row of the stadium seats with several of my classmates, prior to the start of a game, when a rock came sailing right by my head. I yelled down to a group out in the street that I was coming down there if that should happen again. This older kid could hardly pick up a rock fast enough and sailed that missile right at us. I was stuck, and whether I liked it or not, I was headed down the stadium steps followed closely by my supporters. A fight began, and I can remember hitting my head on the door of a Ford coupe. It sounded like a base drum when I hit. I knew I was in for it, but managed to get on top long enough to get in a couple of punches before they pulled us apart. There was the ritual handshake, and it was back to baseball. We later became good friends, having developed a mutual respect for one another. He didn't throw rocks, and I was careful about making brash statements.

Rough Riders
Front left: Tom McGill; Front right: Horace

All About Horses

There was a lottery in town. One of the prizes was a Shetland pony. Tom was the lucky winner, and it was exciting to watch as a stable was made for his new horse, Prince, behind their garage. This pony was far past being a thrilling ride, but he was a good pony to learn to ride on. One day, Tom and I were riding bareback on Prince and suddenly we began to tilt a little bit to the side. We ended in a heap, and Prince just kept on going to the stable. Tom wasn't too eager to let me ride with him after that.

Mr. Osten from across town had a beautiful riding horse, which he rode in parades. It was a "paint," with brown and white markings in big splotches, and it was big. He had a small pony for his daughter Alma Mae, and he told Dad that I could ride it whenever I wanted, as it needed the exercise. I would ride my bike across town, saddle this Daisy, and back to our neighborhood we would go. This little pony was lacking in the horse-power department so I was always bringing up the rear when Bob Siminsma, Tom, and I would ride out on a back road at the north edge of town.

Leo, the man who picked up our grass, lived across the street from the school. He was in a dying business with his stud horses; tractors were replacing the need for farm teams and their renewal. He also dealt in horse trading and bought worn-out or sick horses to be shipped to Omaha and processed into dog food. It became almost a ritual for my friends and me to go over to the corral to see what had come in. One day I got there late, and the gypsies had traded a pony and colt. A couple of the kids said they had ridden the colt named Lightening and that I should try. I got on, grabbed the halter rope, and said to let go. Lightning took off across the corral and headed right for a hitching post in the middle of the area. He planted his feet, lowered his head, and sent me sailing right at the hitching post. I went flying by the post, and that's as close as I ever wanted to come to leaving this planet. No one was very successful in riding Lightning; he knew he had the upper hand. About a half-mile from the stable was his limit. Past that point, he began to sidestep, rear, and paw. He had the last word.

The Tree House

In the summer, my classmates and I liked to climb trees. The founder of the city had the presence of mind to plant elm trees along the boulevards in the residential areas. These were not the towering elms found in the eastern part of the state, but were prairie trees that never got more than forty feet tall. They dripped a sap that would damage the paint on any car parked beneath them. They were not revered, as the nickname "piss elm" testified. They were not good for climbing because the branches formed such narrow crotches that one could get his foot stuck quite easily.

We found that the best trees to climb were the box elders. The bark was not rough, and the branches provided nice perches where we could sit and speculate on everything from religion to girls. We were always on the lookout for branches whose crotches could be fashioned into slingshots.

There were some simple tree houses put together, but none could compare with the one I had devised in the elm next to the garage. The contractors who built our house had made a ladder out of two-by-fours. It was about twelve feet in length and about two feet wide. I discovered it one day in the rafters of the garage and soon had it up in the elm between four sturdy branches and about sixteen feet in the air. The ladder was inverted, so it was no trick at all to lay some planks between the legs for seats. I had to make steps up to the bench by nailing small boards to the tree trunk. As time went on, I was able to construct a back and then a shed-like roof. The floor space was expanded so that one could enter through an opening from below.

My friends were always welcome to visit and all was going well until one Sunday afternoon. Richard Richter was sitting in the tree, and I was standing on a support board with my upper half leaning through the opening. I hadn't changed my Sunday shoes, which had leather soles. The next thing I knew, I was flat on my back between the curb and the sidewalk. A startled "Rick" looked down. "Are you all right?" he asked.

Well, no. My left arm had caught a nail and was laid open from inside the elbow to six inches toward my wrist. I could see muscle where the skin had parted but no blood. Dad had me lie on the floor with my arm up in the air, and he called for Mom to come down from upstairs. She thought

we had company and so put on some lipstick and powdered her nose. She came breezing through the living room and about passed out when she saw me on the floor. Dad put a sterile wrap on the wound, and we headed for the hospital in Le Mars. He did a nice job of sewing me up, and there was no muscle damage.

I was riding my bike down the sidewalk a week later using no hands, and I lost it. I skidded up on someone's lawn, my healing arm taking the brunt of the fall. I powdered the green grass stains on the bandage to hide them, and when Dad removed the stitches, he was disappointed to see how the wound had seemed to spread. Much later, when I related what had happened, I think he was relieved to hear the facts of the matter. The tree house was gone in a day. The trees came down with Dutch elm disease and they were gone, too.

Above: the family in Rock Valley, Iowa
Below: Brother Peer, age three;
Father Lester, age forty-two; Horace B, age ten
1939

The Drum and Bugle Corps

The baseball program ended with the war taking attention away from local events. The men were leaving for military service. It seemed appropriate that we children should be marching, too. The American Legionnaires came up with a complete drum and bugle corps outfit, which included drums and bugles. It so happened that an assistant to the band director of the University of Michigan Marching Band was home visiting his parents for the summer. Norman became the taskmaster of our newly formed corps.

There were well over eighty of us ranging in age from eight to eighteen, and it was soon determined who played what and where one stood in the ranks. The baton twirlers and the high-stepping "whiz" all had one thing in common—their dads were in the Legion. The drum section led the group with the buglers bringing up the rear. My teeth weren't suited for playing the cornet, but they were fine for playing the bugle. We were outfitted with bright blue caps that covered the head but had no bill. They could be folded and stuffed under the belt. Our shirts were white with long sleeves. The pants were white duck, and a red satin sash tied around the waist and draped down the right side to the knee. Black shoes completed the uniform.

Norman laid out a set of rules that would have made a Marine drill instructor blush. Practice started at nine and ended at twelve. "Don't be late and no talking in the ranks." If one missed a practice without a good excuse, he could be dismissed. It was serious business with him, and he was to take raw material and make a precision marching corps in one short summer. We did rear marches, right and left flank moves, scattering into formations, and regrouping, all the while blowing on the bugles and rattling the drums. Norman was very particular about our staying in step.

A performance was scheduled for early August in Hudson, South Dakota. Two stock trucks outfitted with benches transported us the fourteen miles to Hudson. We straddled the benches so they wouldn't tip going around the corners. The last seven miles were on gravel so the dust was everywhere, but no one seemed to mind. It amazed me that we managed to get through our intricate maneuvers, and folks said it was well worth the price of admission. A week later the grand performance was held in Rock Valley, and there were over two thousand spectators. Norman soon returned to the university to obtain a doctorate in music. His rules had carried the day, and that was the end of the Rock Valley Drum and Bugle Corps.

School house, Rock Valley, 1930s

More Music

Soon after we moved into the new house in the spring of '36, a truck pulled up to the front door and an upright piano was installed in the dining room. It was a Vose & Sons from Grandma Erickson. Palma had played on it at the farm and at the town place. I began taking piano lessons from Margaret Bolser. She was a competent teacher, but I had not entirely bought into playing the piano so progress was really slow.

School superintendent McNally's wife took over my training. She thought I would grow out of the bad habits I had formed. The lesson was at half past nine on Saturday morning in her home. Mr. McNally was tolerant of having his Saturday morning interrupted, but I didn't blame him for being a bit gruff, which seemed to be his nature anyway.

One Saturday a few of my friends had planned an early morning fishing hike to Tommy Collins Lake about a mile from the edge of town. I went along with the idea that I would be back in plenty of time for my lesson. We had fished for an hour with no luck when suddenly I got a bite and reeled in a small carp. Having actually caught a fish changed my concept of the passage of time. It seemed important to me that I should catch more fish, especially since I was having all the luck.

I glanced up to see a familiar green 1939 Ford bouncing across the field. I hurried over to the car carrying my lone fish on a stringer, and said, "Look what I caught." "Get in," was the only response. There were no other words spoken during the drive to my lesson. With an office full of patients, Dr. Hegg was not in the mood for conversation, and I could appreciate that. I don't know when the message hit me about making a commitment to the piano, but it must have been about that time.

I can't say that my progress at the keyboard was significant. The solution was to locate a male teacher who could act as a role model and who could build some enthusiasm into my efforts to learn to play. My parents didn't have any great ambitions for me to become a virtuoso, but Dad said I would be glad someday for the ability to sit down and play for my own enjoyment.

Mother took me to Augustana College in Sioux Falls, South Dakota, a mere forty-five miles away, where I was to meet my new teacher. Mr.

Eric Strum, a Norwegian from Minneapolis, had aspirations for becoming a concert pianist. He was a nervous fellow and probably not accustomed to instructing an eleven-year-old on basic piano technique for a whole hour. He was also concerned about being drafted into the army. We could have gotten along fine, but he soon enlisted in the navy. I was turned over to Mr. Earl Lee, head of the music department at the college, who would be my piano teacher over the next five years. He had studied with a countess in Italy and was also Norwegian.

One must remember that I had picked up several bad habits in the process of changing teachers and so was barely afloat in terms of the time already devoted to the skill. Mr. Lee had infinite patience with me, but there was a time or two that he simply pounded on the piano keys out of sheer frustration.

My parents soon determined that the old Vose & Sons piano took up too much space in the dining room. Mother wanted a buffet in its place, so they purchased a new Steinway grand piano from The Williams Piano Company in Sioux Falls. It cost a thousand dollars and was paid for in three equal installments. The company delivered the piano and placed it in one corner of the living room, where it set the tone for that room and more or less determined my Saturday activity for the next five years.

My parents assumed that I would practice one hour a day. It usually took me two days just to recover from a Saturday with Mr. Lee. There always seemed to be more than I could master each week. Panic would start to set in the closer we got to Sioux Falls, and I would spend a furious half hour on the practice piano down the hall from the studio. To make matters worse, the young lady whose lesson preceded mine would stand outside Mr. Lee's door exchanging pleasantries with him as she was leaving. Then she would go by me with a smile that seemed to say, "Too bad for you, fella."

Mother would drop me off at the college, then she would go downtown to do some serious shopping. After the lesson, I would catch the bus to the Shriver & Johnson department store, where we would meet for lunch before starting for home. Twenty-nine cents covered the cost of a tuna and noodle casserole dinner, which included a roll and a glass of milk.

Mother drove the car each week, so Dad had to borrow a car if an emergency occurred during our absence. One time, several miles out of Rock Valley, a team of horses pulling a hay wagon came flying out from a farmer's driveway right in front of our car. Mom went down into the ditch, up and over the driveway and down into the ditch on the other side, then back onto the road without losing speed. All the while she glared back over her shoulder at the farmer for not having his team under control.

From the book *Rock Valley Records and Recollections*

*Leo Grossenburg riding roman style
on Harvey and Prince*

Changes in America

When the United States became involved in the Second World War, there would be some major changes in the lifestyles of Americans. Men enlisted or were drafted. The women left the small towns for jobs in the military industry. Many enlisted in the Women's Army Corps, which had its headquarters in Des Moines, Iowa. This was a separate branch of the army, where the women could fill non-combat positions, releasing male soldiers for more hazardous duty. The navy soon followed with women serving in both the Navy and the Marine Corps. Women who flew aircraft were a special group flying combat planes to England as well as delivering planes to training bases. These were often dangerous flights, even without involvement in combat missions.

Sioux Falls became an Army Air Force base with some twenty thousand soldiers stationed in a city of less than forty thousand. Many would be on the streets on Saturdays, wearing their winter uniforms with big overcoats, boots, and stocking hats with the ubiquitous pot helmet perched on top. Their breath was steamy in the cold, and they were on the lookout for something to buy for a dollar or less from their twenty-one-dollar-a-month pay.

There was a shortage of meat, butter, and sugar. The government rationed these items throughout the country so everyone shared equally in what was available. Chicken was plentiful and farmers seldom worried about red meat. Gasoline rations caused the biggest upset. Ration books were distributed, and a stamp from the book would let a consumer buy a certain quantity of the item rationed. A-card stamps allowed the car owner four gallons for the week. Doctors held C-cards, which allowed stamps for additional gasoline. One could save for a trip by not driving for a week. There was some trading of stamps on the black market. Farmers could get gas for their tractors. It had a different color and was not to be used in their automobiles. They were on the honor system, and it was bad for that color to show up in the farmer's auto tank.

Rationing created a dilemma concerning my weekly trips to take piano lessons. The solution was to provide a bus service for any lady in town who wanted to ride with us to do her shopping. Sometimes we would have four ladies riding along. The speed limit was reduced to 35 miles an hour to conserve on miles per gallon; those rides became all day affairs.

Brother Peer began taking lessons from Miss Cox, who was a well-regarded piano teacher in Sioux Falls, which helped justify using the gas. I eventually found the lessons more meaningful and improved my skills to the point where I could consider playing in the state music contest held in the spring. I chose to play Chopin's "Prelude in C-sharp Minor." I thought I had it pretty well memorized, but there was a part at the end that was very much like a part in the middle. I would come to that part during the contest, and then I would be back in the middle. After a couple of rounds, the judge blew his whistle, and I got out of there. No superior rating came out of that.

I was not discouraged, so the next year I played "Clair de Lune" by Debussy. The contest was held in Sac City. They dusted off an ancient Steinway concert grand for the occasion. The action on this piano was so heavy that I could hardly get a sound out. I got through it this time, but the critic was not kind. The baseball season was postponed a whole week, so I could play the piano in the contest without having swollen hands from catching the ball at first base. I had to go back to Mr. Lee and explain to him that I had botched the job. He was sympathetic, and I really believe he was proud of the way I played that number for him. Years later, a national piano competition in his name would be held annually at the college.

Boy Scouts Rock Valley, 1940
L. to R.: Rich Van Eldik, Jack Riley, Horace, Raymond Schutz

The Outdoorsman

The Boy Scout movement became popular in Rock Valley about the time I was old enough to be a scout. It seemed like just the kind of activity my friends and I could relate to. We had already spent a lot of time out at the Rock River and had even taken our blankets to sleep all night in the woods. We would go to the meat market where Hein Kosters would give each of us a couple of hot dogs to cook along with the can of vegetable soup from home. One time we shot a pheasant, cleaned, and roasted it. It wasn't very good, so we got some cowlick salt from the pasture to season the meat, but that didn't help. Being a Boy Scout seemed like a natural thing. We got uniforms and started going to the meetings.

Our scoutmaster was the Methodist minister. He planned an overnight trip to the Sioux River where we would set up camp, spend the night, and fix our own meal before returning to Rock Valley. I was the bugler and was allowed to stay in the big tent with the scoutmaster and a couple of senior scouts. When morning arrived, I would be given the signal to blow reveille and summon the campers to the headquarters tent to start cooking. Reverend Rachey was having a hard time getting to sleep, so he finally pulled the seat cushion out of his car to cushion the bumps in the ground that were keeping him awake. I wasn't getting much sleep either, so when it came time to blow the bugle, they had to wake me. All the campers were ready and waiting for the bugle to sound. It was cold, and I was half-asleep. The noise I made didn't sound much like reveille, but it was enough to bring everyone running to the tent.

We were to make our own stew, which would include an assortment of vegetables and some meat. We were all very hungry by the time our stews were ready. "Baldy" had an extra-large cooking pot, so he took longer to fix his stew. He was going to have the best stew of the lot. When it was finally ready, he placed the pot on a log while getting his eating utensils. In the meantime, Hale came running up the path eating a banana; he didn't see the stew pot; his foot caught the pot and sent it flying. Baldy just sat down and cried; he was so hungry, and there was no back-up food. Our scout days ended when the minister left to go to medical school, but we had learned to tie some useful knots in the meetings.

During the war, hunting pheasants, ducks, geese, squirrels, and rabbits in season was a popular pastime for my chums and me. Game was plentiful as most of the game hunters were off to war, but there was also a shortage of shotgun shells. The farmers didn't seem to mind if you hunted their land as long as you asked permission and they thought you could tell a cow from a pheasant. It was not unusual to see a flock of a hundred or more pheasants in the fencerow along the side of a country road.

The opening of pheasant season meant that the men teachers and the superintendent let off school early. Some of us students would accompany them through the cornfields to drive the birds up in the air, where they could be shot. Eugene and I seemed to have picked the best row because we fired as fast as we could load. We didn't hit a single bird but it was great fun.

Ray and I were duck hunting the river bends one day when a flock of Canada geese flew over our heads and landed on a small lake just beyond a hill. Ray had a .20-gauge pump shotgun, and I was equipped with an old .410-gauge shotgun, which I had to carry just right or the worn firing pin would get stuck and the gun wouldn't fire. We planned to duck down and run, while in a crouch, toward the lake. We would get up on the geese before they could take off. Never mind the farmer across the lake who was waving at us so he could get in position to shoot, too.

We came up to those geese and Ray's shotgun sounded while mine just went click. The firing pin jammed! Ray's dog, a golden retriever, jumped into the water after the goose. When he got to the bird, the goose whacked him with its wing; Ginger beat a retreat to shore. We waited for the goose to drift to shore, and then headed for home with the prize. I discovered that the barrel of my gun had a chunk of mud stuck in the end. It was my good fortune that the firing pin jammed or I could have blown the end off the shotgun or worse. Ray's mom roasted the goose and invited me over for the dinner.

I acquired a single shot .20-gauge and went duck hunting along the Rock River one day. One could spot a flock of ducks on a bend in the river and then circle up on the high bank side to be in position for a shot. I tried this strategy noting that I was alone except for two horses at the far side of the pasture. I made my way up to the high bank walking slowly, then crouching down, then on my hands and knees, and then crawling to get a bit closer. Suddenly I had the feeling that I was not alone. I rolled over to see this horse standing within a foot of my legs. I jumped to my feet; the horse reared and let out a snort while the flock of mallards took off to safety. The horse was curious about my being in his pasture.

Hale hunted by himself on Saturdays while I was taking piano lessons. He had only twelve shells to last the whole season, so he was very careful not to shoot unless he was certain to bring down game. Sometimes he would hunt all afternoon and not fire a shot. "Not close enough" was his motto. One day we were hunting together and a pheasant came within range. We both fired and the bird took off rising high into the air. It suddenly set its wings and came sailing right back toward us. We opened fire and the poor bird was shot into tiny pieces. We looked at each other as though to say, "What did you shoot for?"

One day my neighbor, Rick, said his dad wanted to shoot a pheasant for supper. I went along to see how this was done. Rick had a short barrel .22-caliber rifle. We would drive slowly along a country road until we spotted a rooster at the edge of the cornfield. Rick would roll down the window and plink the bird in the head with the rifle bullet. This was illegal on several counts, but worked fine until Rick shot a hole in the floor of the car while we were driving along.

I once shot a merganser, better known as a fish duck because of its diet of fish. Mother roasted it, but it was a pitiful sight when she brought it from the oven—shrunken down like an Egyptian mummy. We weren't big experts on matters relating to cooking wild game!

Uncle Albert Erickson's farm, east of Burr Oak, Iowa

Mickey the Dog

Our relatives lived far enough away that a visit from any of them meant an overnight stay. With only two bedrooms, any company was to have the master bedroom. Dad would sleep on a cot down at the office, and Mom would take the sofa in the living room. We had no motel worthy of the name, and the hotel was for permanent residents only.

Mother's cousin Selma Mallom and her husband, Carl, were on their way to the Black Hills from Decorah, and they planned to stop for a visit. They were bringing a dog. When I heard this, I had to make a place for it on the stair landing leading to the basement. They arrived, and the dog, Mickey, went right to the box on the landing and seemed to say, "This is the place for me." The little rat terrier looked like the dog Dad had when he was a boy, which I had seen in pictures. As they left, it was announced that Mickey was to stay. Some kind of negotiation had taken place, but I can believe that the trip to the Black Hills got a lot less expensive for Selma and Carl.

Mickey led a pretty carefree dog's life. There were no leash laws in Rock Valley, and Mickey followed Brother Peer around wherever he went. Unfortunately, Mickey ran afoul of a big Irish setter in front of the corner drugstore and barely escaped with his life. Dr. Meerdink, the veterinarian, had to stitch his throat together where the big dog had torn into him. He was not the same after that experience. He had a forlorn look, as though we had somehow let him down. He began to chase cars, and one day a local delivery boy chased him into the curb with his truck, and that was the end of Mickey. I buried him in the garden. Mother and Peer were too grief stricken, and the only solution was to get another dog.

Peer was now old enough to go fishing at the river. The new dog, also named Mickey, went fishing with him. Peer came home and told me that the dog had swallowed some liver he had been using for bait. He said the hook was in the liver, and that he had cut the line. I saw Mickey running around the yard showing no ill effects and thought no more of it. A couple days later, I noticed that someone had apparently tied a string around his tail; the tail came up but the string didn't move. I recalled little brother's story, so it was a trip to the vet with me holding Mickey's head and Dr. Meerdink working on the other end. Mickey bit me a few times during the ordeal, but Dr. Meerdink got the fishhook, which was caught just before the exit. It had gone all the way to the end.

Our nearest relatives were a couple of hundred miles from Rock Valley. Dad's family, his mother, Oliva, brother Clarence, and children Dorothy and Clifford lived in Harmony, Minnesota. Dad would leave at 2:00 A.M. to be on his way to visit them in Harmony, and would return later in the day. He never felt comfortable leaving his practice for any length of time. It was unheard of that he should make the social rounds that Mother considered necessary. She had learned early on that she would have to go it alone when it came to visiting, and she accepted that.

Dad was always glad to see anyone who made a trip to see us. He even took the tonsils out for three cousins during one of their visits! I came home and Jean, Jerrine, and Tom were lying in my bedroom after returning from the surgery in Hudson, South Dakota. The ice cream that was promised wasn't even a comfort at that point!

I was five when my tonsils came out. Earl Bergsma, who was fourteen, had his out at the same time. It was Earl's fourth and last time. This was done in Hudson, because that was where the dentist who administered the ether had his practice. I can remember giving him a kick in the stomach as I was going under.

Years later when I was in boot camp in the Marine Corps, our platoon was marching on the parade ground, and the drill instructor called a halt and ordered me to step out of the ranks. There was Lieutenant Commander Earl, who had come to see how I was getting along. We had a nice visit while the platoon stood at ease. Then it was back in the ranks, and off we went for another hour of marching drill.

Brother Peer, age four, and Mickey, 1940

Back to Burr Oak

At least once a year Mom, Peer, and I would board the train in Rock Valley for a trip to Calmar, Iowa, near Decorah. Either Uncle Bill or Uncle Albert would meet us there and take us to his respective farm near Burr Oak. Burr Oak is now famous for having been the place of one of the Wilder family homes in the book *Little House on The Prairie.*

Uncle Si's family, including Jean, Jerry, Tom, Karen, and Kristen, would come from Saginaw, Michigan. Uncle Bill and Hilda's children were Marcella and Phyllis; Uncle Albert and Florence's children were Shirley and Norris; Uncle Carl and Alma's children were Myron, Esther, Vernell, and Hildred; Uncle Sherman and Eleanor's children were Lynne, Nancy, and Sigrid; Uncle Leif and Ida's children were Sherman and Donald. Not all could be present at any one reunion, but eventually a tradition was established which has carried into the twenty-first century.

When the brothers got together, there was only one agenda: Norwegian Whist was the game, and everyone but Otto considered himself the top Whist player of the group. It is doubtful whether they could name all the nieces and nephews or if they considered that a problem (you couldn't tell for sure), but they would nod when you came around the table. Mother eagerly joined the game and asked no quarter and gave none when it came to competing. The wives were at home with Mother, and she with them, so she really enjoyed reunion times.

One of the most memorable times for me occurred while we were staying with Uncle Albert and Aunt Florence. Jean, Jerry, and Tom were also staying with us at the farm that night. The following morning, the families were to make a trip to Uncle Carl's farm located on Bear Creek several miles down the road. Aunt Florence was noted for her pastry baking; her doughnuts especially were highly regarded. On this occasion, she decided to supplement the menu with some bakery cream puffs. These were the real goods, and Tom and I finished off what was left of them for breakfast that morning. Just before we were to leave, I realized that I was not well and headed for the outdoor privy. I knew this was not going to be a good day, but I had to get in the car since I could not be left behind. Two miles down the road the car had to be stopped, and I was out in the ditch throwing up my breakfast and the cream puffs. I looked back and saw that the car Tom was riding in was

Cousin Don Erickson was a casualty of World War II.

stopped too, and he was out in the ditch. We got to Uncle Carl's; Tom and I spent most of the day lying on a blanket under a shade tree.

This was a day that I should have been bonding with Carl's children, but my only recollection of them was their hiding behind some trees, peering out at us. Perhaps they were afraid that we had some contagious disease. We recovered as the day wore on only to be confronted by a cloud-bursting rainstorm that sent Bear Creek roaring out of its banks. We had to cross the bridge over the creek to get out of the valley. Water was over the road leading up to the bridge. Uncle Otto was dressed in his white suit and was not about to wade so Norris, Tom, and I walked ahead of the car to determine if there was a washout in the road.

Mother, Peer, and I would go up to stay with Oliva and Dorothy out at the Hegg farm for a few days. Grandma Oliva was short and petite and full of energy. She fixed Norwegian dishes and gave me my first taste of fried blood, which was made up into a casing something like a summer sausage. Cousin Clifford put me on a big white riding horse, and I would gallop this horse down to the main road and back up the lane to the house. Cousin Dorothy looked after Grandma Oliva after she fell and broke her hip. Oliva was bed-ridden for seven years; Dorothy lived with her and was her main caregiver. Dorothy had a special place in Dad's heart.

My Uncle Leif had moved to Saskatoon, Canada, and his youngest son, Donald, had joined the Canadian Air Force at the start of the Second World War. After his training had been completed, Don was sent to England as the navigator on an American-made plane called the Hudson. He was part of the crew patrolling the Irish Sea when the plane crashed. There were only two survivors; his station was in the nose of the plane, and he could not save himself.

After Don's death, Mother felt that she should go visit Leif and Ida, so one summer day we boarded a Great Northern train in Sheldon, Iowa, and rode to Minneapolis, where we stayed the night at the Radisson Hotel. The next morning we began an all-day train ride to Winnipeg, Canada. We stayed overnight at the Fort Gary Hotel, which was owned by the railroad and was the showcase of a chain of hotels across Canada. The landscape across Canada was dull, so I suppose the railroad made it up to the traveler by making the overnight stay something special. The next morning, we boarded the Canadian Pacific and were on our way to Saskatoon. The train was packed with French-Canadian soldiers who took a shine to Brother Peer, who made them laugh. I wonder what he thought—they didn't speak English! The train was so crowded that we would spend an hour in line to get into the dining car. The meals were worth the wait, however, and our servers waited on us with a linen napkin on the arm.

Leif and Ida were very appreciative of our visit. They had pretty much reconciled to the fact that their son had given his life in the line of duty. Leif had a pretty good job with Robin Hood Mills and traveled around the territory. He talked constantly about the advantages of living in Canada, but I think he missed the life around Burr Oak. Cousin Sherman was a reporter on the *Saskatoon Daily* and was not eligible for military duty because of a bout with rheumatic fever as a child.

Sherman took me golfing a couple of times. The trees on the course were Canada cherry scrubs. If you hit a ball into them, you could forget about finding it. I rode Sherman's thin-tired bike out to the air-training base. Student pilots were practicing landing twin-engine Cessna planes that were painted a bright yellow. As I stood in the road with the bike, the pilot and his instructor would fly over the road about thirty feet over my head. They were so intent on the landing that they hardly noticed me. I was ready to dive into the ditch if one of the planes flew too low.

After a stay of several days, we were on our way back to Iowa.

Family reunion at Bill Erickson's farm, 1940. L. to R.: Sherman, Albert, Peer, Carl, Palma, Otto, Silas, William

Juvenile Adventures

There was always something for a pre-teenager to do in Rock Valley. An abandoned sandpit north of town was made into a public swimming area, complete with bathhouse and a raft as well as a shallow area for non-swimmers. The 150-yard wide pit was spring-fed. The raft could accommodate twenty sunbathers and a few of us who tossed in stones and dived for them. We did that to show off our swimming skills. We didn't find anything unusual about swimming to the far side and back even though parts of the pit were thirty feet deep. There was no lifeguard on duty. The inevitable happened one afternoon when a young boy went in right after dinner, before anyone else had arrived. Everyone thought he probably got a cramp and drowned. After that, interest in the sandpit waned, and it eventually became a waterfowl preserve.

Our little gang would ride our bicycles to other towns. One such trip was to Fairview, South Dakota, thirteen miles one way on gravel. The balloon-tire bikes had only one speed so we did a lot of walking on the uphill slopes. It was worth the trip though because the last mile wound downhill and into the valley of the Sioux River.

We loved to ice skate in the wintertime. The first skates I owned were clamp skates that attached to your shoes. They were pretty clumsy affairs, not very sharp and prone to falling off. When hockey shoe skates became available at the hardware store and the town provided an ice rink near Main Street, there was often a pickup hockey game with three or four players on a side. During one of the games, one of the players got hit in the mouth with a hockey stick and had to go home. His father came out on the ice after the high stick; it was the first time I heard a preacher cuss. Other days would see us heading for Benson's Hill east of town. We would sled and ski until dark and then walk the mile-long trip back to town.

There was no roller-skating rink in town; we learned on the sidewalk. These skates were hard on leather shoes. The clamps fastened around the toes of your shoes and a leather strap held the heel in place. Near our house, a particularly smooth run of sidewalk stretched the whole block and was a popular skate area for the neighborhood kids. We would make scooters out of the wooden crates that oranges came in and discarded roller skates.

One could expect standing water along the streets after a rain in the spring. It was great fun to ride through the puddles on our bikes. In the winter, when they froze, we skated on them. We learned the meaning of "rubber ice," when the ice would bend with one's weight but spring back if you kept moving. It was thin ice anyway you looked at it, and you could be counted on to get wet up to the knees before the day was out.

The streets were not plowed in winter, and we took advantage of the farmers who came to town. We would grab the back bumper of a car and get into a ski position, riding all the way to the outskirts of town. I'm sure some farmers wondered why they couldn't get up to speed. The buckle overshoes didn't last more than a couple of days of this, and the clothes we wore took on a greenish cast from the exhaust.

Sundays were quiet days for me. Dad would be down at the office, making the rounds of his patients in the hospital at Le Mars, or seeing some who needed daily care in their homes. Mother would be singing in the Methodist Church choir while Brother Peer and I sat in the back row of the church. Sometimes folks around us would get little brother laughing, and we would have to sneak out the side door when the sermon started.

There was no television in those days, so I had to read a book or find something to do outside. I would take my baseball bat and hit rocks into the neighboring field. I became very good at this, although the bat got pretty well chewed up. After I graduated from high school, "Solly" Schemmer, the town baseball team manager, asked if I would suit up with the semi-pro team that had been reorganized. One of my duties was to hit fly balls to the outfield during the pre-game warm-up.

I learned to drive the car on Sunday afternoons. It was a stick shift 1941 Ford so I had to learn to coordinate the clutch with the gearshift. I had 150 feet of roadway along the east side of the house to practice on before coming to the end of our lot. I could get up a pretty good speed and then swing into the garage and slam on the brake, then I would back up and do it all over again. One time I came a little too close to the side of the garage door; this left a streak of white paint on the side of the fender. A little green crayon over the white streak solved that problem.

Dad didn't attend church: I think it was because he didn't want to show preference for one denomination over another. There were eleven churches in the community, and he provided his services to the priest, the ministers, and their families free from any fees. Dad and Mom were brought up as Norwegian Lutherans. One day they decided that I should begin Lutheran confirmation and should be attending Sunday school and church. Peace Lutheran was seven miles south of Rock Valley; one day Dad took me there in time for Sunday school, and said I was to go to church, and he would pick me up afterward. I was eleven years old and was expected to know what to do in any given situation.

I went to the Sunday school and then waited a half-hour for the service to begin. I sat in one of the pews while the church was filling and noticed the women sitting on one side, the men on the other. Reverend Beyer began the service, and it was the one Sunday a month when he gave it in German. The liturgy, hymns, sermon, and the prayers were all in a foreign language. This was something that I had not figured on so I soon got out of the pew and left the church. This meant that I would have a good hour before Dad would come for me. I reasoned that it would be helpful if I were to start walking toward Rock Valley. A car came along, and I got a ride for a couple of miles, and then another car took me a little further. I eventually walked up on our yard as Dad was getting into the car. It was almost one o'clock—my shoes were pretty much shot. He was miffed that I had altered the plan that he had laid out.

However, I returned the next week and soon became acquainted with the kids at the church. I found out that several would be attending high school as my classmates in Rock Valley; they were very good students coming from the country school. Dad was often late coming for me. I got pretty good at identifying the sound of the Ford while it was still more than a mile away, and it was always a good sound.

As I got older and obtained a driver's license, the folks would let me drive out to Luther League on Sunday night. One spring evening the gravel road was too soft to travel, so I decided to go to the road a mile west and then south for seven miles. I had the '41 Lincoln that had sixteen-inch wheels. It was not a good car for traction on bad roads, but I seemed to be getting along all right until I went through a mile-long intersection only to find that I was now on a mud road instead of gravel. I thought if I could just make it up the little hill, I would be on the downgrade for the rest of the mile, then I could get back onto gravel. Halfway through the mile I started up another hill and knew I was going to be stuck. I got out of the car and looked around. Total darkness! I left the parking lights on and started walking the way I came. It didn't occur to me that there would be no cars down this road that night so I could have saved the battery by leaving the lights off.

I reached a farmhouse and called Dad to come get me. He said I should call the farmer, who lived on the corner near where I was stuck, in the morning, to ask if he could pull me out. Monday morning came and I called the farmer. Dad took me out to the farmhouse, and I knocked on the door. The farmer invited me in, and said he was finishing breakfast, so I sat and watched him finish eating in silence. Finally he turned and asked what I was doing there. As I was about to explain, I looked out the window to see the car being pulled up the road by a tractor. I felt really stupid, because I had called this farmer's brother who lived on the other side of the road. The farmer got a big laugh when he found out he wasn't going to have to pull me out of the mud and his brother got stuck with the chore.

Dad had a keen memory that enabled him to keep abreast of the rapid changes occurring in the field of medicine. He would end the day reading one of the medical journals, and once he read something, he could quote from it. He would remember patients' birthdays or anniversaries, even if he hadn't seen them for several years. He once told me that he could remember something that was pertinent in the life of each of his patients. He was very good at defining words due primarily to his classic education at Luther College. I would test him at the supper table, and he would break down the word in its root meaning and then define the word. I never bothered to check to see if he was right!

The summer before we entered the Second World War, Dad took up the game of golf. He had gone to Omaha to see about military service as a doctor, but told them he wasn't going to go around inspecting toilets. The military board must have decided he had plenty to do in Rock Valley with patients from five surrounding towns. The practice had grown so that he needed some recreation that would get him away from the telephone for a few hours, and golf was one answer. The nearest course was located in Sheldon, Iowa, twenty-five miles east of Rock Valley. Several men in the community got the golf bug at the same time. The group included Dr. Jim Schroeder, Jim Vanderploeg, Dr. "Mac" Schutz, and "Hein" Kosters.

A small river ran through the nine-hole course. I went along to stand along the riverbanks to prevent golf balls from going into the river. This seemed reasonable enough until Dr. Jim hit a walloper, and the ball began to curve toward me. I ducked as the ball shot right over my head. After that episode, I got a golf bag and four clubs and was soon able to play as well as the men. It was exciting to be with these grown-ups just to hear them converse.

If a baby case were pending, Dad had to decide if it was worth the trip to the golf course. It happened more than once that the phone at the clubhouse would ring to summon Dad as we got in the door; we would hop back into the car without any golf that day. It was customary for the group to run to the first tee just to try to get a little golf in before that phone would ring. The folks at Sheldon would say, "Here comes the Rock Valley slice," when our group would appear. Dad truly loved the game although he never was able to hit the ball straight to his target. Its flight was like a big banana, always to the right. But he could chip and putt and would give the better golfers at the club a run for their money.

New golf balls were not available to the public during the war. One could send a dozen old balls to the factory, and in a couple of months, they would come back with new covers. One day Mac discovered a dozen U.S. Royals on the shelf at a hardware store in Fairview, South Dakota. Even though they looked a little yellow, he was excited about the prospect of hitting a new ball off the first tee. He took a big swing, and the ball shattered into a hundred pieces! We all had a good laugh, but that incident so disillusioned him that it wasn't long before he gave up the game.

One evening we played a few extra holes with the local golf professional. We thought we were the only folks on the course. It was the custom in those circumstances to play across fairways from the fifth tee to the first green to be able to finish near the clubhouse before it got too dark.

The pro hit his drive and then it was my turn. As I started to swing the driver, I saw two golfers step out from the seventh tee, which was concealed from our view by trees. Instead of hitting the ball where I was aiming, I pulled it to the left at this fellow. I yelled "fore," and he started to turn but the ball hit him right on the head. He was flat on the ground, and we rushed down to him.

I thought he was dead, but he started to get up as we got to him. The ball had struck him on the upper part of his ear. The fellow said he was all right and wanted to continue playing. Dad insisted that he get to the local hospital and have an x-ray. It turned out that he did have a slight fracture of the skull. Dad paid his bill!

This was the only time I have hit a person while playing golf, but I did manage to hit myself with a golf ball. I was practicing in the backyard by hitting balls into a canvas I had hung on the clothesline. This worked pretty well until the wind came up and the canvas would flap in the breeze. I found a cedar post and placed that at the bottom of the canvas as an anchor. I decided to hit one last shot and swung a little harder than usual. The ball squirted along the ground, hit the post and flew back, hitting me on the nose. I heard the ball drop a few seconds later, and my nose felt like someone had tweaked it. There was no blood, no broken nose, just a tweak. This was as close as it comes to not being around anymore. I took the canvas down and decided never to attempt that again.

Horace, sixth-grade basketball

Working on the Farm

Dad got me a job working as a farm hand two miles east of town. Judson and Francis Smith welcomed me more as a friend than an employee. Fran was a Norwegian from the neighboring town of Doon. They were a young couple with a family, which included baby twins. Judson was a good mentor for me; he loved to talk about farm problems, politics, and the language idiosyncrasies of his peers. I suspect Dad may have offered to pay my wage, which turned out to be $2.50 per day. This was important pay for a young man about to enter high school.

My first task was to learn to drive the Allis Chalmers tractor. Judson still had a team of horses, but it was only a matter of time before the tractor took over all the chores. The corn was up about six inches when I was assigned to cultivate the weeds out from between the rows. I had to pay strict attention, because it was easy to get into a row and either take it out or cover the plants with dirt. The hardest part of the job was getting the tractor through a low spot in the field without getting stuck.

In the early forties, farmers raised hogs, beef cattle, milk cows, sheep, and chickens. They planted corn, oats, barley, flax, and hay. The main tasks during the summer were to feed the animals and deal with the crops as they matured. Judson went to the local creamery once a week to get whey for the hogs. He had several oak barrels by the hog pen, and it was my job to slop the hogs. I loved the smell of the fermenting whey, and the hogs would go wild trying to get a place at the trough. I would pour two-gallon pails of the stuff into a trough. They were all over each other trying to be the first to get filled. The squealing, snorting, and the smell of the hog yard and the fermented whey were sensations that one didn't easily forget!

There was a real hired man on the place. Pat had farmed but lost everything in the Depression. Now, he was content to being a hired man working with the horses and livestock. I saw him only at mealtimes. Pat had an interesting way of approaching the food on his plate; he would take his fork and stir everything together before beginning to eat. During the lunch hour, he often entertained us with stories of his farming experiences.

Stories of a pack of dogs running at night concerned everyone; Judson had a pointer mutt on the place and worried that it might be one of the pack. I came to work one morning to find him upset that the sheep were not down from the upper pasture. We started to look for them and came upon the first one lying dead near the fence line. We could see that the flock had been chased all around the field; there were dead sheep to mark the path they had taken. Sixteen had been killed that night, and to make matters worse, the pointer had been seen with the pack. He had to be shot because he could not be broken of that pack instinct.

When it was time to cut hay, Pat brought the horses out to pull the mower. The team pulled the hay rake through the field to turn the hay into long rows to dry in the sun the next day. Judson would hitch the team to the hay wagon, and the horses would move slowly along the row as we pitched the hay onto the wagon. The horses seemed to know just how fast to pull the wagon, and a voice command from Judson was seldom necessary. Ropes were laid on the floor of the wagon to act as a sling to lift the hay into the barn. There would be three layers on a fully loaded wagon. When it came time to unload, we pulled the wagon up to the barn directly under the loft door. A track extended out from above the door, and the horses would pull the sling of hay up to the track through an arrangement of pulleys. The load would slide into the barn loft where it could be dumped as needed. It was important that the hay was not damp as it could begin to ferment and generate enough heat to cause a fire.

On one particular day, we had almost filled the wagon, when suddenly, out of a nearly clear sky, a lightning bolt struck nearby. A storm was rapidly approaching. It sounded like a freight train just to the south of us. Judson got the horses turned and headed for the barn at a near gallop. We went through a small ditch, and the wagon broke in the middle but we kept going. We reached the barn just before a torrent of rain descended. That day marked the worst tornado damage in Sioux County's history. It created a swath of destruction over a twenty-mile stretch just six miles south of Rock Valley. Many farm homes and properties were damaged, but no one was killed.

Neighbors always helped one another in those days. Threshing the oats was one of those times. A neighbor of ours owned a threshing machine and a steam engine. During the season, Mr. Davison traveled to various farms to thresh the oats. The farmers belonged to a ring, and would follow the threshing machine to help until all the farms in that ring had their crop in and straw stacks formed.

The tractor-pulled binder would cut the oat stalks and tie the stalks into bundles to be left in the field in rows. The farmer and helpers would place the bundles into shocks to dry. When the threshing machine arrived the farmer had to decide where he wanted the straw stack. The machine would be positioned upwind from the stack, and as the neighbors came into the yard with their wagons loaded with bundles, the machine would be started using a steam engine for power. They tossed the bundles into the thresher, and the oat grains poured out one of the pipes into a grain wagon while the straw flew out another pipe onto the ground. In time, a huge straw stack would be formed, which would be used for bedding for the cows and horses the following winter. The fellow who moved the straw around on the growing stack had the worst job on the threshing crew. He wore a bandanna around his face to keep from breathing the dust, but it was always hot and dirty work.

Judson was always ready to help out a friend or neighbor in trouble. One day he got a call that one of his farmer friends was seen doing somersaults naked from the barn to the house. Dr. Hegg had been called and requested the sheriff to accompany him to the farm, as this could be a dangerous situation. When they got to the place, the sheriff wouldn't get out of the car so Dad had to go into the house alone, where he was able to administer a shot of tranquilizer to the poor fellow. Judson and a couple of friends cleaned him up and dressed him, then took him to the hospital in Sioux City for evaluation. Judson was one of those fellows who got a five o'clock shadow by mid-afternoon. When they arrived at the emergency entrance of the hospital, the patient was the only one of the group who looked decent so the two attendants in the white coats grabbed Judson thinking he was the patient. Judson laughed as he told that story!

The farmers took great pride in their horses. Judson would go into the stalls of these big animals and give them a slap to move them over. He would see that they were taken care of after a day's work, and they seemed to know his touch. I could never get the confidence to go into their stalls, and I think they sensed that, and I sensed that it was just as well to stay away from their backsides.

Teenage Years

My high school years were dominated by the entry of our country into the Second World War. From December 7, 1941, when the Japanese navy attacked Pearl Harbor in Hawaii, until the Japanese surrendered to our armed forces in August 1945, the focus of the people was the war effort. I was headed out the front door for the movies that Sunday when the news came of the attack on Pearl Harbor. Dad said, "Horace, you will be in it before it is over." I was twelve at the time and he was close to being right.

As a freshman in high school, I started the first basketball game of the season. We lost to powerhouse Hull 83 to 21, but I was high scorer for our team with 11 points. The following Monday, a team meeting was held and Superintendent McNally, or "Prof" as we called him, informed the team that in the interest of conserving gas for the war effort, the basketball schedule would be cancelled. I offered a car since we had no school buses, but the offer was ignored. Prof had a son who was flying gasoline into China over the Himalayan Mountains so it wasn't a surprise that he felt strongly about wasting gas.

We eventually formed a pretty good team. During my junior year, we had an eight game winning streak going when we played Ireton. We won the game only to learn soon after that the opponents had all come down with the mumps. This was distressing news for our team, especially when we heard that the two game officials had the mumps too. One by one, several of my teammates came down with this childhood disease. I can remember looking in the mirror for three days straight before the inevitable swelling began. I had mumps on one side and then on the other! Prof came for a visit. I must have looked like a tree stump, because I remember him laughing at the sight of me. Our team entered the county tournament with five members of a twelve-man squad. Three boys were added so there would be someone on the bench. They said the team received a standing ovation.

The high school had two athletic programs during the war. Baseball was played in the fall and spring and boys' basketball during the winter season.

My junior year in basketball had ended and spring baseball was soon under way. Eight games were scheduled with other schools in the area. We were undefeated and ready for the first game of the sectional tournament. We thought we were pretty good as our group had received summer instruction from a former professional ball player. We watched the Yankees' and the Cardinals' World Series games, which were shown on the newsreels at the movie theater, prior to the showing of the main feature; we took on some of the mannerisms of our favorite players. One observation was that they chewed tobacco as they played the game and the bulge in their cheek signified that a chew was in place. They could also spit the brown juice farther than one would expect spit to go.

John Bauman, senior and best athlete on the team, found that a mouthful of raisins was a good substitute for the chew. He was the runner on third base during the first game of the tournament and had the raisins in place. I was the batter, and Coach Gorzeman signaled for the squeeze play, which required the batter to bunt the next pitch, and John would come running to home plate for the score. I was a pretty good bunter and so this play seemed sure to work. However, I had somehow confused the squeeze bunt with the sacrifice bunt, which was designed to advance a runner on first base to second base to be in a position to score. The batter in this instance would bunt only if the pitch was a strike.

The pitch came in high and inside, and I let it go for a ball. John was coming to home plate with a full head of steam, only to be confronted by the catcher holding the ball and ready to tag him out. He was able to avoid the tag by turning around and running back toward third base. John was now caught in a "hot box" between the catcher and third baseman. He was determined to avoid being tagged out and persisted in running back and forth on the base path all the while chewing vigorously on the raisins. Fatigue was setting in, and the first sign of it was a trickle of raisin juice running down John's chin. As he began gasping for air, the raisins escaped down his chin in greater amounts. He finally crossed home plate with the score as the defense collapsed. His uniform shirtfront was pretty much covered with the raisin juice and saliva.

We cheered the great effort, and John was all smiles at the outcome of the squeeze play. He gave me a look in passing, and I was glad he had scored the run, as it spared me some impromptu instruction. Coach Gorzeman later informed me of the proper squeeze play role of the batter, but he had to laugh as he recalled the spectacle. Young John went on to become a professional baseball player. He could hit the fast ball with the best of them, but the curve ball was another story.

A high school student's social life in Rock Valley consisted of going to the movies, eating hamburgers at the restaurant, and listening to the radio shows. The Movie Theater was the most glamorous part of our lives. A musical usually played Sunday, Monday, and Tuesday. Wednesday was Bank Night, when the wining ticket might win $40 or $50. Friday and Saturday featured a cowboy movie and a B picture. The couple that ran the theater was from California and had a Hollywood connection. They acted the part in manner and dress.

The husband, Mr. Bogarde, played the xylophone and may have been in vaudeville at one time. A cousin of his came to town and gave professional tap-dance lessons down at the hotel. Mom signed me up, as she didn't want me to miss any cultural opportunities. My neighbor and good friend Bill Rozeboom took lessons too. He was two years older than me and caught on to the instruction pretty well. I was growing fast and my feet had a hard time keeping up with the music. Mother got me to perform a routine for relatives on Uncle Albert's front porch once during one of our visits, and I felt like a fool. Bill and I were the only students this fellow had, and he soon moved on.

Red's Cafe was a popular night spot after a movie or a basketball game. The Joy Lunch was another stop off for me. I would go there right after basketball practice and order a shake and a chili dog to hold me until supper. The shake was filled to the top of the can, and the chili covered the whole plate—all for a quarter. Sometime later, on my first day working the sandwich bar at the University of Iowa Union, I made a shake for a student, which got the attention of the manager who exclaimed, "What are you trying to do? Break us?"

When I got old enough to borrow the car, I could also take a trip to Perkin's Corner for a chocolate shake. One night, eight of us piled into the old Lincoln, whose engine had recently been overhauled. I couldn't get the car to go any faster than fifteen miles per hour. I started with a full tank of gas, and when we finally made the eight miles to Perkin's, the gas gauge showed half full. The return trip was no better. The next day the garage man discovered the air cleaner was plugged with dirt. He said I had put about ten thousand miles on the car that night. I should have told Dad, because the car engine fell apart right after we traded it.

Some of the popular radio shows of that time: "Jack Armstrong the

All-American Boy," "I Love a Mystery," "Fibber McGee and Molly," "Jack Benny," and "Bob Hope" and his theme song "Thanks for the Memories." Dad never liked Jack Benny; I couldn't figure out why at the time. I later realized that it was because they looked so much alike, and Benny wasn't a very good actor in the movies he made.

Because of the cancelled basketball season, Friday nights were open, and it didn't take long for the girls in our class to organize parties in homes for those evenings. There would be ten or so at a party, including younger brothers or sisters. We played parlor games, but the chief focus was dancing to the popular tunes of the day. This was important to the boys because they knew that knowing how to dance was necessary when one got old enough to go to the Arkota Dance Palace to hear the big bands and to meet girls.

There was no formal dating among my classmates in those days. It was a lot cheaper to wait until the movie was over, then ask the young lady if it would be all right to walk her home. This happened to me one summer evening during my sophomore year. We got across the street from my "date's" house, and suddenly I realized that I was expected to kiss her. I did this and then took off running down the street, headed for home like it was past my bedtime. I often wondered what she thought.

Dad hinted from time to time that prep school might be a good experience for me. This was an idea that didn't appeal to me at all. Dad did enroll me in an eight-week summer athletic camp at St. John's Military Academy, Delafield, Wisconsin, prior to my senior year of high school. I was surprised to learn of this development two days before I was to enroll at the camp!

The camp offered one hour of military training, and the rest of the day would be devoted to sport activities, which included swimming, golf, sailing, basketball, tennis, track, and rifle target shooting. The staff was made up of college students who were generally highly regarded in their particular sport. Bob Kurland, one of the first seven-foot All-American basketball players, was in charge of the basketball classes. He demonstrated defensive techniques one day in class and called on me to play the offense. I scooted around him. He must have been satisfied that his defensive stance was well tested, and that may have had something to do with my being chosen for the all-camp basketball team. Brother Peer was to go to the same camp several years later and be chosen the "outstanding basket-ball player" of that summer.

Most of the campers were from southern states. It was the custom of many wealthy families to send their children to these camps largely to escape the heat of the southern summer. There was a girls' camp associated with St. John's, and their activities were similar to those of the boys. The age groups ranged from eight to eighteen, and many of the campers would return summer after summer.

I was a late admission to the camp and was assigned to a dormitory room in DeKoven Hall. Most of the campers lived in tent cabins situated near Lake Nagawicka, which was still part of the school campus. Monk, my roommate, and I got along very well as we had similar interests in sports.

Paul Brown and his wife lived right in the dorm area to supervise our camp unit. They were responsible for seeing that we behaved and that we kept our rooms clean. The evening meals were served family style; the Browns were always served first. One evening we had Canadian bacon as the meat portion of the dinner. When the plate came to me there were three pieces left. I took all three—they were small pieces—and suddenly realized that the two campers next to me were without any meat. I had forgotten about meat rationing, so I put the two slices of bacon back on the plate, and I sat red-faced.

The noon meal was informal and campers and staff sat at random. This meant that there was a certain amount of rowdyism, and it was difficult to control. A couple of campers found that a butter pat on the end of the knife could be made to reach the ceiling. One of the boys decided to attack the person across from him by firing a butter pat in his direction. The target ducked, and the butter pat went on to the next table, striking Mr. Coffey, the long-time tennis instructor at Oklahoma A & M, behind the ear. He spotted the guilty party, got out of his seat, and came around the table to the young man. He took him by the shoulders, shook him vigorously, then proceeded back to his table, sat down, and removed the butter pat from behind his ear. I thought it a very appropriate response to the situation.

At the camp, we spent one hour each day in military drill. They issued uniforms and organized us into companies with the tallest in the first ranks. I was a squad leader and marched at the head of the first column. We had dummy wooden rifles and were to learn the manual of arms. One Saturday morning while waiting for the weekly parade to form, our company was standing at ease, which meant no talking in the ranks. I had to say something to the recruit next to me and suddenly an "officer" was in my face berating me in unflattering terms for talking while at ease. These "officers" were graduated seniors at the military school and were there to teach us military training. I took a sudden dislike to this fellow for what I thought was excess verbiage on the matter. Imagine my dismay when, on my first day on campus at Grinnell College two years later, I met this same individual coming toward me on the sidewalk. He didn't recognize me so I was able to get by him without renewing any unpleasantries. Rumor had it that he left school under dubious circumstances shortly after midterm.

During the last week of camp, a historic event occurred. On August 5, 1945, the atom bomb was dropped on Hiroshima. There was a general feeling of relief that the war would soon be over. Few of us had any inkling of the consequences of that military action. We weren't sure of the meaning of an atom, let alone the concept of splitting one.

The war had left its mark on our class. Lois Kooima's older brother Lawrence was a pilot flying B-17s. One day this bomber flew low over Rock Valley. It was a salute from Lawrence, who was on his way to England to join the Eighth Air Force. One day months later, Lois ran crying from the school at the news that her brother had been killed in a flight over Germany. It was a sober day for us.

Bob Riley, a classmate, joined the marines as soon as he was seventeen. Word came that he had been killed on Iwo Jima, the Japanese island that was captured by the marines and gives us the famous picture of marines raising the American flag atop Mount Surabachi.

My senior year in high school brought many changes in our lives. Gas was no longer rationed, automobiles were being manufactured again, servicemen were being discharged from the military service, teachers were coming back from service to claim their jobs, and we got a new superintendent. His name was Mr. Haas, and he would also be the basketball coach. To my surprise, he was the man I had visited with during a tournament at Rock Valley when I was in eighth grade. I remembered how patient he was in talking with me about his team and basketball in general. I was thrilled that this man would be my coach for at least one year. Unfortunately, we won only five games that year, but gave a strong showing despite losing thirteen games.

Basketball shoes made during the war were not worthy of the name. They were made from imitation rubber and left black marks on the floor of the gym. The floor would be completely black after a season of play, which upset the custodians. The shoes provided little traction so the players spent most of the game slipping and sliding around. This contributed to low scores and a conservative style of play. The two-handed set shot was considered appropriate if one couldn't make a lay-up. The game soon evolved to the running-one-handed shot, which was soon replaced by the one-handed jump shot and the one-handed set shot. Coach Haas got me a pair of Converse shoes with only two games left before the tournaments began. I was very quick in these new shoes, but the soles of my feet were blistered so badly after just one game that the season end was welcomed.

Mother had become an active volunteer in the community after Brother Peer started school. When she was the county chairperson of the Red Cross, she was able to get soldiers home on leave in emergency situations. She and a couple other mothers pushed for a new high school. She loved raising flowers and looked forward to the annual flower show, eventually judging at shows around the county. She was also a hostess to Republican candidates campaigning in the area. As president of the Iowa Medical Auxiliary in 1954, she traveled around the state encouraging the formation of new chapters. She helped found a young women's club in Rock Valley, a group which was instrumental in uniting the community to build a swimming pool.

Dad had little time for community service other than his medical practice. He did belong to the Rotary Club and was often asked to speak at the weekly Monday noon meetings. There was always a program of some kind. He told me of one program and Reverend Jones's magic trick. The Reverend claimed that he could take a scissors and cut off the necktie of a person, and then restore it to its original condition. The bank president was seated nearby, and with one motion, the Reverend snipped his tie right in half. The joke came when he was unable to restore the tie, and so the favorite tie—given as a gift by daughter Cassie—was finished. A month later the news was that Reverend Jones was preaching at a Methodist church somewhere in South Dakota.

Dr. Lester Hegg was voted Rock Valley's first Man of the Year in 1954, and Palma Hegg was voted first Woman of the Year in 1955.

During my senior year in high school, I was elected president of the class. The first class meeting was held, and I proceeded to conduct the meeting in the manner in which we were accustomed. Professor Haas was present, and it soon became apparent that business as usual was not going to work. Robert's Rules of Order were to be followed to the letter. The rest of the school year was more or less a blur as far as being president was concerned.

Graduation came and I was to give a speech at Commencement. This was a momentous time with world peace on everyone's mind. I couldn't think of a single thing to say, and so in desperation, Miss Norris, my English teacher, dragged out a speech from her files. Mother was in the hospital with pneumonia at the time, and I would practice this speech as I drove down to see her. Penicillin made her stay a short one, and I administered her shots after she came home. Commencement came and neither parent was there to hear me struggle through the speech. It was just as well!

Rock Valley High School baseball team, Spring 1945
L. to R. back row: Dick Van Eldik, John Bauman,
Richard Richter, Horace Hegg
Front row: John Harmsen, Hale Pember, Bob Potts, Bernard Wissink,
Ken Bonthuis, Coach John Gorzeman, Manager John Van Maanen

Rock Valley High School basketball team, 1946
L. to R. back row: Manager Lonnie Lewis, Leo Buckley, Leonard VerMulm,
Eugene Vanderwell, Horace Hegg, Ray Schutz, Donald Kaskie.
Middle row: Junior Kooima, Junior Benson,
Bob Potts, Hale Pember, Cuno Ranschau
Front row: Cheerleaders Mary Ellen De Smet, Eloise Miller, Betty Lou Benson

I began to think about college. Most years one could write for an application, and if the grades were decent, it was just a matter of time before you would be accepted for the fall term. I sent for ten applications in early June and had only one response. Grinnell College sent me an application, which I filled out, and by the middle of August was accepted for the fall semester. Because of the returning veterans and the GI Bill providing financial aid to the servicemen, most of the colleges in the state were full to the rafters. Grinnell had apparently been so selective that they were in danger of coming up short. It was fate that I should apply and be accepted at such a late date. I'm sure the admissions director scratched his head over that one more than once!

Seven from our graduating class went on to college and all finished with liberal arts degrees. Some went on to attain advanced degrees.

Graduating Seniors, Rock Valley High School, 1946

Part 2

Stepping Stones

Alumni Recitation Hall
(The ARH)
Grinnell College

Grinnell College

Blair Hall Science Building
(no longer standing)

The fall of 1946 found me boarding the train at Hawarden, Iowa, heading for Des Moines, where I would spend the night. A bus would take me to Grinnell the next day. My steamer trunk would follow, so I carried a suitcase, newly purchased, that had a collegiate look about it. I got to Des Moines to find that a convention was in town and the hotels were all booked. I asked the desk person at the Hotel Fort Des Moines for help, and he said he could put me up in one of the private party rooms. They put a cot with bedding in the room for the night, but I had to be out of there by 8:00 A.M. I awakened to the noise of the bus boys preparing the room for a morning event.

I arrived on Grinnell's campus after a forty-mile bus ride, and got my suitcase into my assigned room at Smith Hall by mid-afternoon. Hugh Acton, also a new arrival, suggested we go to the fieldhouse to check out football gear. Never having played high school football, this idea hadn't occurred to me. I was the seventy-second person to check out a uniform that day. What an auspicious beginning to a college life!

I recall that my first forty days on campus were a source of benign comfort. I was involved in football practice and the Centennial Play, in which I was cast as Mr. Hill, the gentleman who plunked down a dollar to start the college in 1846. Classes seemed quite interesting, and it was getting-acquainted time.

Grinnell College, a well-regarded liberal arts school, was known as "The Pioneers." Women were welcomed as students almost from the founding days; physical education was another pioneering element. Fraternities and sororities were never a fixture at Grinnell; students were assigned to halls and cottages, which functioned as social units without the problem of exclusivity.

"Prepping" was still practiced and served the function of getting to know upperclassmen, even if it meant a swat on the rear at house meeting night. Punishment was meted out for walking on the grass instead of the sidewalk or for not wearing the beanie cap, and other things of that nature. It was also common practice for the preps to make a 9 o'clock food run, for any upperclassman in the hall, to the White Spot, a hamburger joint just across the road from campus. In the fall of 1946, this could mean that a twenty-three-year-old veteran of the Battle of the Bulge could be hotfooting it for some nineteen-year-old sophomore! The veterans that I knew were good sports about prepping, but it is an interesting concept when you think about it.

Prep Week culminated in a one-night assignment. Leonard R. Leonard, a future roommate, and I were given the task of getting a horse up to the third floor of Dibble Hall. We proceeded to make rubber shoes out of some old tire inner tubes, and then went to a stable near the campus and stole a horse. We came back to the campus with the horse and led it up the steps to the first floor near the door to the housemother's suite. The horse left a calling card by her door, and we suddenly realized that we might be able to get the animal up the stairs, but could we get it down? We got the animal back to the stable just as a car came driving up the lane.

One of Grinnell's most illustrious graduates (1949) stole a pig under similar circumstances, and it was only the supreme effort of his mentor, Dr. Grant Gale, that kept Robert out of jail. Robert Noyce went on to co-invent the microchip. He formed Intel, which became a leader in the electronics industry. He was a huge benefactor of the college with a gift of Intel stock. I hate to think of what would have happened to us if we had been caught as horse thieves. I believe we thought these assignments had been cleared through some higher authority.

Grinnell College was celebrating its centennial in 1946. A play had been written that covered the important events of the college. It was an ambitious undertaking requiring a cast of over seventy. If you had experience in a drama of any kind, you were qualified to be in the play. I had been in a couple of disasters in high school, but guilt by association was not a warning flag. It should have been! Marcus Bach, professor of Religious Studies at Iowa University, wrote the script. There were six scenes requiring three sets to be placed on a temporary stage in Darby Gym. The sets were on casters so they could be rolled into place behind the curtain.

My role as Mr. Hill was significant as he gave the first dollar to start the college. As I recall, there wasn't much for me to say after I got rid of the dollar. The tornado that almost destroyed the college was one of the unique features scripted into the play. Dress rehearsal found all members of the cast sharing the football locker room as a dressing room. This was news to me!

A full house of some fifteen hundred guests eagerly awaited the unfolding drama the night of the performance. The curtain was to open at 8:00 P.M. At 8:45 P.M., the first scene began, while in the background one could hear the paint sprayer finishing the second set. One of the unforeseen problems was changing the sets after a scene. The temporary stage was too small so a set had to protrude out through the curtain to make way for the passage of the set it was replacing.

At the end of one scene, J. B. Grinnell, the founder of the college, was portrayed dying while sitting in a rocking chair. John Thompson, one of several students who actually had some acting talent, was playing this role. There were delays between scenes, and the person in charge of the curtain didn't cue John so the curtain opened in the next scene to an empty chair. He dashed out to the chair quite alive and began dying again. Mr. Bach was in the dressing room by this time, and there was no consoling him. The play was beyond recovery, and folks in the back row were bailing out; we got to see a lot of haircuts as the evening progressed. The final curtain closed to about a dozen diehards at around two o'clock in the morning. As far as I can tell, there is no record in the Grinnell College literature of this event ever taking place.

Dad had given me some advice about how to study in college. He advised, "Don't take the easy road," and, "Don't waste your time in bull sessions getting ready for exams." There was an internationally renowned figure on campus teaching the course International Relations. Joseph Dunner was on Hitler's black list, and so Dr. Guillermo Mendoza, my counselor, suggested it would be interesting for me to take his course; I agreed. I also enrolled in a course called The Bible as Living Literature. I thought this would be right up my alley as I was a confirmed Lutheran.

Dr. Dunner announced before his first test to "be brief with one's answers," as he didn't want to have to read more than what the answer required. I filled only the first page of the blue book, which must have been a new record for an eight-question essay test. I remember answering one question with the word "Church." My paper came back with the notation "too brief!" I got a 76 percent—60 was passing. I took the Bible course a little too lightly. Imagine my surprise when my first test score came back as a 46 percent. "Who was Yahweh anyhow?" I improved to a respectable 78 percent by the semester's end, but the 46 percent went home to Dad and Mom, and I'm glad I wasn't there when that arrived! The second semester ended on an upbeat note, and I was ready for a summer of relaxation.

The Packinghouse Job

A friend of Dad's had found me a job for the summer. Bob Morrow was a pharmaceutical salesman from Sioux Falls, South Dakota. He was a great golfer, and would call on Dad late in a day, then they would head for the golf course. Bob said he could get in to see Dad easier than any other stop on his territory, even though he had to wait his turn like any patient. He arranged for me to work on the icing gang at Morrell's Packing Company in Sioux Falls for the summer. I was to start the following Tuesday morning.

I got to the YMCA on Sunday and immediately began checking the classified ads for a room to rent. I had to get something close to a city bus line, and only one ad met that criterion. There was a phone number and instructions to call after five. I wanted to get to them before anyone else called, so I got out the phone book (Sioux Falls had a population of about forty thousand at that time) and made it to the M's before I found the number. I got the address and on Monday afternoon was waiting at Mr. and Mrs. Mulhauer's door when they arrived home from their wallpaper store. They were surprised to see me, as they had given no address in their ad.

When I said I would be working at Morrell's and would be getting up at an early hour, they were reluctant to rent the room to me. The previous tenant had worked at Morrell's and had made too much noise leaving so early in the morning. I promised that I would put my shoes on only after I left the house, and so they relented. This was a big relief for I had no car and could not see living out of a suitcase at the "Y" the whole summer.

Mr. Anderson, the foreman of the icing gang at the plant, briefed me on the various duties and gave me a quick tour. The primary task of the icing gang was to load the bins with ice at both ends of the boxcars being readied for shipments. This was done by filling huge buckets from an overhead chute, and then pushing the buckets on rails overhanging the train of cars parked below.

There could be several rows of cars to be iced, and we could switch the buckets to the proper track. The switches had to be returned to the main lines or the buckets would go off the track on down to the ground. It was an awful sound when those buckets started hitting the ground. We also washed the boxcars to clean the accumulation of soot from the coal-burning engines so they were a bright orange and looked brand new. When home for the weekend, I would see the train going through town, and there would be the boxcars heading for the big city filled with meat products that I had helped keep cool.

The worst job on the gang was making the ice. This was a one-man job, which consisted of pulling three hundred-pound containers of ice from the brine floor with an overhead hoist. These Popsicle-like containers were then transferred six at a time to a vat of boiling water where the ice blocks would be freed from the metal container; tipping the whole works so the ice would slide down a chute into the cooling room. The hard part came in setting these blocks on end.

The semi-pro baseball team had been reorganized after the war, and I was in my second summer with the team. I was the local "talent" and filled the utility backup on the team. If one of the players failed to show up on Tuesday, I would play right field. Orin Crider, Bob Tucker, and Tony Koenig drove down together from Sioux Falls, so I rode with them and got an earful of baseball lore from those trips. Solly, the manager, had me buy the week's supply of bats from Dauby's Sporting Goods in Sioux Falls.

One night we played a town from West Central Iowa. The Stille brothers were the strong features of this team, and one of them pitched the whole game. This turned out to be one of the longest games ever played in the history of baseball. Dad left in the eighth inning to deliver a baby girl in Canton, South Dakota, twenty miles away; when he returned to town, he was surprised to see the lights on at the park, and came to watch the 21st inning. It was two o'clock in the morning when we scored the winning run.

It was a quiet ride back to Sioux Falls. We arrived just in time to go to work. I looked forward to my afternoon nap that day. Because I got up at five each morning, when the alarm went off at 5:00 P.M., I started to get into my work clothes. What a feeling of relief that I still had the evening before me.

The summer passed by and I signed off on an interesting job. Mr. Anderson said I could come back and work for him again.

More School Days

I managed to fall out of another tree in our backyard. It was an apple tree. I hit my crazy bone on a branch, lost my grasp, and down I came. Polly looked out the kitchen window to see me lying under the tree apparently dead. She rushed out shouting, "Horace! Horace! Are you alright?" Earlier that day, I had driven a lady to the Le Mars hospital in the old Lincoln. Oil fumes from the engine were leaking into the car interior so I was a bit groggy by the time I returned home. Mother wanted some apples from our tree, and in my woozy condition, I was ready for a fall.

My only injuries were some chipped front teeth in my lower jaw. Dr. Schroeder said that he would smooth off the jagged edges for the moment, and we should wait to see what developed.

It was time to go back to Grinnell College. Some college friends were on the train when I got on board at Canton, and we started a bridge game. I bought a ham sandwich from the train vendor and took a big bite of it. To my dismay, I could not chew my way through the ham because of my newly chipped teeth, so I sat for a good five minutes with that sandwich stuck in my face while my playing partners looked on in wonder. I couldn't open wide enough nor could I pull myself free from that ham.

My first experience with bridge had come during a card session in the Smith Hall lounge. Bob, Stan, and Skip were sitting at a table and needed a fourth to get the game going. They insisted that I sit in, even though I had protested that I didn't play the game. They couldn't believe that a college student would be that ignorant, so I said something about having played a lot of cards and I sat in. The dealer was at my left; he passed, my partner passed, and the third hand passed. I thought this was easy, and I passed too. Stan said, "I don't have anything. What have you got?" The same response came around the table to me so I showed them my hand. One look at my cards and the three got up in disgust; there would be no bridge game with this fellow. To this day, I have the feeling that the hand dealt me was the best bridge hand I would ever see, and I had no idea. Now I was interested, so I began to kibitz in the lounge and eventually was able to defend myself.

One of my roommates at Grinnell had initials that formed the acronym GAS. We would not think of calling him Glen; there were other Glens, but there was only one "Gas." He was a first-rate basketball player for the college and so was well-known around the campus. One day he got a package in the mail from his mom. It was a supply of midnight snack goods including crackers, cheese, and ham. I had one small helping, but Gas was hungry. We made seven trips to the bathroom that night, and I held the wastebasket for him. I wasn't in such great shape myself. The room was spinning around when I went to lie down. The doctor finally came toward early morning and decided that the crisis had passed. It was the talk of the campus for a day or two. The package with the ham must have been delayed in the mail room for a few days. Experiences like those are what bonding is all about

Richard Overholtzer from Ida Grove was my roommate for three years. He was a Younkers' scholar and had to maintain an 88 percent average to retain the scholarship. This was no problem for "Rich," until he took Professor Bauman's Modern European History class. His semester grade was eighty, which was a shock because his test scores averaged in the low nineties. He pointed this out to Dr. Bauman, but the semester grade was to stand. I had a similar experience with Dr. Bauman except my test scores averaged eighty and I received an eighty-five for a final grade! I had made a couple of wild guesses during class discussion that seemed to have pleased Dr. Bauman and figured that must have been part of the equation.

On the basis of this one comparison, I boasted to Rich that I would top his best efforts the next semester. Dr. Bauman had made one concession to Rich about the grade discrepancy. If Rich would act as Dr. Bauman's foil in class discussions, challenging some of the professor's outrageous interpretations of history, it was implied that things would go well for Rich in the second-semester class. Rich responded that he wouldn't have any part of such a scheme. The semester ended and Rich received 100 percent for his grade. He never mentioned my little presumption. I wasn't even close to winning that wager.

Jim, Rich, and I shared a suite my senior year. You could tell Jim Kissane was going to be a college professor after just visiting with him for a bit. He had a way of unfolding a story so each word would have been the most appropriate that could be found. His parents were teachers and imparted a sense of learning in him without the least bit of ostentation.

Jim was good at basketball, but he loved tennis. He also had been a baseball pitcher in high school and had a good throwing arm. One day he was throwing the football in the gym and the football coach spotted him. "I want you out for practice tomorrow," he said. This idea so intrigued Jim that the next day he went to Darby gym and checked out a uniform. By the time he figured out how to get it on, the rest of the team had gone. He joined a group and began to do the calisthenics drills. After some time, a coach approached him and asked if he was with the college team. He had accidentally joined the high school team that was also practicing in the general area. Somewhat daunted by this experience, he got to the right practice area just in time to get in line for the tackling dummy drill. He told me his back folded like an accordion when he hit that tackling dummy. The next morning, Jim couldn't get out of bed, and when he finally got to his feet, he headed for the equipment room and checked out of his football career.

Those four years following World War II were unique in the college's experience. Many of the students were veterans whose ages ranged from nineteen to fifty. Their experiences and maturity were different from what one normally would expect from a typical student body. Some of the men were returning to Grinnell to finish their degrees. Others had taken advantage of the GI Bill, which provided money for veterans to get a college education. There wasn't much talk about war experiences, but you could generally tell a veteran by the khaki clothing that was a part of his wardrobe.

John Shoemaker was a veteran who came to Grinnell with a mission for his senior year. He made it a point to have a date every night of the school year. He would shower about five o'clock in the evening and come down the hall wrapped in a towel—singing all the way. It was either a dinner date or something later. He never asked the same girl for a second date, but South Campus came to expect his call, and it got so they wanted to be part of the dating game. John was truly one of a kind and a perfect date, I presume.

The intramural sports program was an important part of the social life of North Campus. Touch football, basketball, softball, bowling, wrestling, swimming, and golf made up the year's activities with competition between the seven halls an ongoing thing. Somewhere along the way, I acquired the nickname "Ace," short for Horace. Even my professors got the hang of it. To this day I have to deal with this nickname in circumstances relating to the college days, but I use the name Horace, because Dad picked that name for me.

Grinnell had no baseball program right after the war. This was fine for me. I could continue playing with the semi-pro team during the summer. By the third year, I had become a regular and played first base. We had a catcher by the name of Johnny Breeze who was the property of the Chicago Cubs. He could make more money playing the semi-pro circuit than he could in the Cubs organization. Johnny loved to throw to first base in the hopes of picking someone off, and he exercised this at every opportunity. He also would run up the first base line to back up any play to first, which was pretty impressive at the time.

We had a pitcher named "Lefty" Swift. Lefty had a lot of guile and a little curve ball but nothing resembling a fast ball. He made a move to first base that was always a shade away from a balk, but it was effective when he could get away with it. One time a base runner stepped about a foot off the bag; Lefty got the ball to me as this guy blinked. I put the tag on him, and he never moved. He just stood there and said, "I'll be damned." One night the Max Lanier All-Stars came to play, and Lefty was pitching. This group was made up of Major League ballplayers who had broken their contracts to play in the newly formed Mexican League, a promotion to bring professional baseball to Mexico. This league didn't last the year, and they were banned from ever playing in professional ball in this country as a punishment for disaffecting. They traveled about the country playing teams like ours. It didn't take them long to figure out Lefty's pitches, and the trees behind the outfield fence were battered with home run balls. Lefty would come back to the dugout after a tough inning, bubbling with confidence that his curve ball was really working.

Another team that got to Rock Valley that third summer was the Kansas City Monarchs, an African-American team. Satchel Paige was in his late forties and was paid $500 to pitch three innings. A crowd of 3,000 was on hand for this game as this was big-time competition, and we thought we were a pretty good team. Satchel grooved the first pitch to Jimmie, our third baseman and the youngest of the three Snyder brothers who played for us. He hit it right out of the park for a home run. Satchel continued to groove the pitches, and when I came to bat there was only

Above: Horace in his dorm room, studying for finals
Below: Grinnell College intramural softball game, December 1948
Jim Heiny, left, "out by a mile." Right, "Ace" making the play

one out and two were on base. He threw a strike and I let it go by; he threw another and I swung and missed; he threw a third strike and I looked at that and went back to the dugout. The next batter was the pitcher and Jimmie was on deck. Satchel took a look at him and promptly walked the pitcher on four straight balls. Jimmie fouled off ten of his best pitches and finally hit a line drive to a leaping shortstop to end the first inning. The pitcher who replaced Satchel was also too fast for us. He was only sixteen and had an older brother, Dan Bankhead, who pitched for the Dodgers. We lost 10 to 4.

I helped our manager, Solly Schemmer, put away the bases, bats, and scoreboard numbers after the game, so the players had gone by the time I got to the shower. To my surprise, Satchel was still there taking a shower. I never said a word to him. I think I likely passed up the interview of a lifetime. Later that summer, he joined the St Louis Browns and had a couple of good years. He was one of the all-time great pitchers in baseball.

By the end of my third year at Grinnell College, I had decided that I would like to become a teacher. I needed to take some preliminary courses in order to get into the education program my senior year. This meant summer school, so I enrolled at Colorado College the summer of 1949. The plan was for me to drive Mother, Brother Peer, and a friend of his to the Black Hills, and from there to Colorado Springs, where Mother would take over the driving to Aspen, Colorado. Dad would join them there for his first vacation since he began his practice.

Aspen was the site of the celebration of Goethe's three hundredth birthday. Dr. Albert Schweitzer, world-renowned humanitarian, would speak about his medical practice in Africa; the Minneapolis Symphony and other notables would also be present for the festival. Aspen would eventually become one of the sought-after places to live for those who could afford it, but at this time it was relatively unknown.

Mother was faced with driving in the mountains after a week of being a passenger, and the experience of going over Loveland Pass was something she would talk about for some time. Dad flew into Glenwood Springs, and he let Polly do all the driving while in the mountains. The rationale for his coming to Aspen was to hear the famous Dr. Schweitzer. They had tickets for his speech, but when they got to the tent where he was to speak, they were asked for an extra two dollars. The celebration had not drawn the crowds that the promoters had expected so there was the extra charge. Dad refused to pay it, and went to the car where he stayed until the lecture was over. Mother was not so principled; she sat through the lecture, which was in French, and she didn't understand a word.

The highlight of my summer in Colorado was joining four students from the college to climb Pike's Peak. We started in the early evening and planned to be at the top by sunrise. A restaurant was at the top, so we hoped to hitch a ride down with some tourists who would have driven there. We had talked to some students about the climb, and they said to eat a very light meal before starting, as one could get sick from the altitude and the climb. We were a cold and hungry group when we finally struggled into the restaurant at the summit. We had miscalculated our arrival, but were able to say we saw the sunrise from near the top of Pike's Peak. We lay down on the floor by the cash register and went to sleep. The air is thin at 14,000 feet, so it didn't surprise anybody that we would be lying there snoring away.

The two young women in our group were able to get us rides down the mountain. I rode with two couples from Brooklyn, New York, and sat in the front seat between the two men who were puffing on cigars. The wives kept pleading to be careful and not go over the edge of the road. The way I felt, I didn't care as I was about to get carsick. They had to stop the car so I could get out to lose my breakfast. They were pretty good sports about the unscheduled stop.

Summer School at Drake University

I graduated from Grinnell College on June 5, 1950. I was in the summer school mode by this time so I enrolled at Drake University to take ten semester hours of organic chemistry. It was an eleven-week grind from 7:30 A.M. until 4:00 P.M., five days a week for eleven weeks. I lived in a rooming house with five graduate students who were taking subjects in school administration. They were GI veterans and had discovered the way to get on the teacher's good side was to buy her a gift. They spent a considerable amount of time shopping for the right gift to achieve the desired result.

One evening they had a brush with the law after partying at a favorite tavern. "Cannonball" tossed an empty beer can out the car window, and it hit a police car. When the officer began writing the ticket, the offender exclaimed that he couldn't do that because they were Drake graduate students. The five of them had to be bailed out of jail at 2 o'clock in the morning by the dean of the college.

Semester finals occurred just before the long weekend of the Fourth of July, and I was studying hard when "Beanie," my roommate, came home late in the evening. It was raining hard. He asked if I wanted a beer, put the can on the dresser, and opened it. The beer squirted out of the top and onto the ceiling. When I got back from the five-day break, Mrs. Horstman, the landlord, met me at the door and said she had good news. "I noticed the roof was leaking in your bedroom, and so I had a new roof put on while you were gone." It would not have been good for me to tell her what really happened.

During that summer, the Korean conflict broke out with the North Koreans crossing their border into South Korea. Beanie wanted to re-enlist right away, because he could sense the trouble our soldiers would face. He eventually became a school superintendent in northeast Iowa.

The outbreak of the Korean conflict—the government would not call it a war—put a new outlook on my future plans. I was at the age where I could be drafted into military service at any time. My immediate goal was to continue taking courses, which would lead to a teaching position.

Preparing to Teach

I registered at the University of Iowa in September. Hale Pember, one of my boyhood chums, was studying pharmacy at the university. He roomed at Market Manor, a rooming house near the Student Union. He said there was an opening at the Manor and I could work a part-time job at the Union. Rent at the Manor was seven dollars a week; it was close to the chemistry building, and the Student Union was just two blocks away.

The Union was the center of much of the social activity on the campus. Situated on the east bank of the Iowa River, the River Room provided a commanding view of the river. The main floor was composed of a large central lounge, which could be used for a dining room and seated about eight hundred guests. There were several alcoves for small group meetings, as well as a music-listening room. A snack bar adjoined the River Room, which provided seating for up to three hundred patrons.

I worked in the snack bar; my boss was Mrs. "B." She had been with the university for many years so you listened when she wanted something done. Mrs. "A" was in charge of the cafeteria downstairs, and we bus boys could be assigned to duties in either place or to help with large dinners as they were scheduled. We wore white pants and jackets so one knew immediately that we were part of the staff. We worked two hours each day for two meals in the boardroom. Any time we worked more than two hours, we would be paid fifty cents per hour.

On the night of the medical students' dance, I was assigned to the soda fountain, where I would dispense Coca-Cola. I ran out of flavoring by ten o'clock and asked where to find the refill. One of the workers said to look under the counter. There were several jugs of different flavors and a couple labeled Coca-Cola, so I took one of them and refilled the pump. The rest of the evening went by, and when the dance was over, the manager came by to see how we had done. Jack looked out on the tables and could see that things were not what he had expected. Every table had four drinks completely filled. "I've never seen that before!" he exclaimed. We looked at the jug I had taken for the flavoring refill and written in pencil on the coke label was the word vanilla. It was interesting to me that no one complained about the taste of the drinks. "Rat" Brewer, the head bus boy said, "I told you that would happen if some new guy got on the pumps." Writing the name of the flavoring in pencil on the coke label was not a good idea!

The Greek organization dinner was the big event of the year for the Union management. All fifty bus boys would be involved— setting up the tables, serving the dinner, and cleaning up afterwards. Some of the senior help decided it would be a good time to ask the management for a raise. After three days of negotiations and much wringing of hands, management granted a nickel raise.

One fellow prided himself on his busing capabilities, so when we began to clear the tables, "Andy" made a point of stacking his tray very carefully so as to get the maximum number of dishes on it. This began to draw the attention of the student guests, as he had to go through a swinging door carrying this tray to leave the dining room. The load was heavy, but he got it to his shoulder and out the swinging doors with no problem. The kitchen was down a flight of stairs. A huge crash was heard as "Andy" took the first step down. Loud cheers and clapping accompanied until the last teacup hit the floor. The profit for the dinner went down the stairs with the replacement of those fine dishes.

Hale and I used much of our leisure time playing table tennis at the Union. It was good, cheap entertainment. Hale became a defensive specialist, and I preferred the attack game. His defense usually prevailed, but we could put on a good show. There was always someone on campus that could play better, so we could stay humble without much prompting.

Part 3

Measured Steps

1952

Private Horace Hegg, U.S. Marine Corps
Top row: sixth from left

The Draft Board

The year at Iowa ended, and I still needed to take the semester course in practice teaching. The military draft was going to take precedence, and I would have to wait until September before the draft board in Sioux County would call my number. I was not interested in enlisting, as that would have meant a three-year commitment to whatever branch of the service I would have joined. Patriotism was not a factor for me as our borders were not being threatened. I had come to understand that there wasn't much good that would come from shooting at people in Korea, but I was willing to accept being drafted.

My neighbor and friend, Bill Rozeboom, was getting a summer crew together and offered me a job. He came out of Iowa State with a degree in forestry and worked for a wood-preserving company. The job called for our crew to treat every transmission-line pole between Sioux City and Storm Lake. We would dig around the pole to a depth of three feet, Bill would smear the pole with the company's tar-like preservative and wrap the pole with tarpaper, and then we would backfill the hole. This was said to add fifty years to the life of a pole so it was important work. We would do fifty poles a day! It was a fun time because we did everything as a team. We bunked together, ate out together, played golf together, and went home to Rock Valley together at the weekend.

We usually worked faster when we got to the last pole for the day. I made the mistake of bending over and shoveling without stopping and managed to overwork a muscle in my back so that I could barely straighten up. I could not sit either, so the ride back to Le Mars was a half-hour of torture. I couldn't get out of bed the next morning so the crew went to work without me. By mid-morning the pain was gone, and I had nothing to do so I left a note and walked to the golf course, where they found me. The guys were a bit suspicious of such a convenient recovery!

We were nearing the completion of our summer's work when I contracted a case of poison ivy. Starting with a small spot between my boot top and pant cuff, my scratching spread the itching until both legs were covered with blisters. At the time, our crew was bunking in a makeshift dormitory in the attic of the fieldhouse at Buena Vista College.

I would leap out of my bunk in the middle of the night to cover my legs with calamine lotion to relieve the itching. The floor took a beating and I soon had to go home; the crew was glad to get rid of me.

It was early December before I was notified to report for military duty. I spent a leisurely couple of months with the family, and then Mother drove me to the OK Cafe in Alton, Iowa, where I joined several other draftees from the area. This would be my first experience with government bureaucracy. We boarded the bus and traveled sixty miles to the induction center in Sioux Falls, South Dakota. By mid-afternoon I was headed for Omaha, Nebraska, on a bus with seventeen newly inducted marines. They swore us in, and the next morning I was put in charge of thirty-one draftees set to board the train for California. This was more authority than I would ever command during my two years in the Marine Corps.

I asked one of the conductors to take us to the correct train and get us on board. We had tickets for seventeen Pullman berths, six bedroomettes, and two bedrooms. I made the assignments and kept the tickets, which I would present to the conductor as he got to my bedroom. A half-hour passed and there was a pounding on my door. One recruit from the Pullman car was excited and exclaimed, "The conductor said we were all on the wrong train!" The conductor had taken most of the group some twenty cars to the front of the train when we finally caught up with them. It was the same conductor who had put us on the train. I don't remember what I said to him, but it wasn't pleasant.

We got settled in for the three-day trip and went as a group to the dining car for the evening meal. The steward was not thrilled to see us and informed me that we should be at breakfast by 6:30 A.M. sharp the next morning. I pointed out to the fellow that we had first-class tickets and expected the same treatment as any of the other passengers. He said that all the military groups had come to breakfast at 6:30. I offered to get us there at 8:00, and he agreed. We had one problem—one recruit, "Chief," was difficult to rouse—but we got to Los Angeles without further problems. I turned over the papers and the group to uniformed marines, who escorted us on the train to San Diego and the USMC Recruit Depot.

The Marine Corps

We got off the train to experience our first taste of boot camp. Two marines were stationed at each door of several green buses that were waiting. They helped us speed up the loading, and when we got seated the first order was to dump all personal gear onto the floor. The bus was littered with toothbrushes, razors, cologne, and anything that looked like it was sharp. There was no talking during this exercise, and we were pretty much cowed by the turn of events. As we left the bus, a sergeant marched us to a dining hall and instructed us to leave our suitcases and personal gear out in the street. Clair Roth, a football player from Westmar College, Le Mars, Iowa, asked, "Who's going to watch the gear while we eat?" The sergeant said, "You are!"

After finishing our meal, we were marched to the barracks, where we were issued sheets and blankets. I was assigned an upper bunk, and it was time for taps. The sergeant said, as he turned out the lights, "When I call 'hit the deck' at 3:00 A.M., I want to hear one thud as your feet hit the floor." I closed my eyes, and the next thing I knew the sergeant was shouting, "Hit the deck." I was on the floor before I got my eyes open. So began the first full day of boot camp.

The Marine Corps was expanding rapidly because of the Korean conflict. In the "boot" training center, they were setting up Quonset huts, new mess halls were being opened, and additional drill instructors were undergoing training. The recruits were called "boots," among other things, while they were in training. Our drill instructor was Sergeant Jednoralski, who soon became Sergeant "Generosity" behind his back. One never addressed a drill instructor by name. It was always Sir. This was his first platoon, so he did everything by the book. This turned out to be a plus for Platoon 472, as drill instructors had a tendency to get short-tempered after they had been through the training cycle a few times.

Our "training" schedule began at the barbershop. Seventy-six of us got through the barbershop, and the entire group was finished in less than ten minutes. It didn't take thirty seconds to get my haircut, and I didn't have to worry about a part for ten weeks. We were bald. Physicals and shots came next, and then we went to the supply depot for uniforms. We were issued sea bags and a pail. The sea bag had to hold everything we owned.

The pail was to wash our "linens." One recruit put the pail in the sea bag first and then filled the bag with clothes. He bounced the bag on the cement floor to settle the load. The bottom of the pail cut a neat hole in the bottom of the sea bag and all his gear popped out the bottom.

At one point during that first day, we formed a marching unit. I was chosen as a squad leader and marched at the head of the first column. We were assigned to two Quonset huts as our barracks, and I was in charge of one of these. This meant that I "got" to turn out the lights and was responsible for seeing that our sleeping quarters passed daily inspection. This relieved me of standing four-hour fire watches during the ten weeks of training, which was a big deal. "Firewatch" was another name for sentry duty, walking a post and sounding the alarm if unauthorized persons appeared.

We were issued M-1 rifles, which we shouldered in all our marching drills. When we attended classes, the rifles were slung under the sides of the top bunks. Our dungaree caps were pulled down over our eyes so we had to hold our heads back just to see the path in front of us. We often marched within a block of the main gate, but when we went home on leave, we had to be shown how to get off the base. We found that recruits never walked; it was always "on the double." A recruit never addressed a marine but waited for permission to speak. We saluted any personnel who was not a recruit.

The daily schedule was filled from 5:30 A.M. until 9:00 P.M. with the exception of Sunday. On Sunday, we could attend a church service of our chosen denomination, and often the DIs would schedule a touch football game with another platoon for the afternoon. Each day we had a half-hour before lights out to write letters home.

The first four weeks were devoted to classes about combat weapons. How to disassemble them and put them back together was very important to being combat ready. The M-1 rifle was the standard weapon; it could be fired as a single shot or as a semi-automatic. The effective range was 600 yards, although a round could travel about 6,600 yards if the rifle were fired at a 45-degree angle. Other classes were devoted to learning how the Marine Corps functioned.

Military history was important, and a sense of being a marine was continually being developed. Much of our time was devoted to marching on the parade ground, called the grinder, located at the center of the base.

It was over a thousand yards long and a third as wide. Often there would be ten or more platoons involved in close order drill at the same time; discipline was established in this way and precision marching would become the norm. There was one exception to this scenario. Convair built the B-36 bomber. This ten-engined "mastodon of the air" was test flown from Lindbergh Field, which adjoined the marine base. When we paraded on Saturday mornings, we could count on one of those planes to come roaring down the runway with the sound waves from all ten engines shaking the ground. Sergeant Generosity would call, "Column right!" and half the platoon would turn; the other half would keep going straight. This was an understandable mistake, and we would not have to lose competition points, but if Sergeant Generosity was unhappy with the platoon for any other reason, it was out on the grinder after dark for an extra hour of drill. He didn't have to see if we were in cadence; he could hear one boot that was a split second off the beat. We would stay there until he got the sound he wanted!

We practiced the manual of arms as part of our parade presence. The manual was performed as though the platoon was one person. Its purpose was a method to deal with the weapon whether the platoon was at a standstill or in marching order. An important function was the inspection of each weapon to determine that it was not loaded. The person in charge of the platoon would take the rifle from you, look in the breech, see that the weapon had been cleaned, and then present it for you to take back. I instructed my squad to take the rifle back as though someone was trying to steal it. Our squad never flunked an inspection.

I had learned the manual of arms pretty well in my summer camp experience at St. John's Military Academy so I was ahead of everyone in the platoon at this skill. Sergeant Generosity would call me out of the ranks to demonstrate how the manual should be done. One exercise with the M-1 included opening the bolt by catching a tang on the opening rod with the left thumb pushing the rod back as one held the rifle at port arms with the right hand. This was easy compared to closing the bolt, which was done on command. One had to stick the thumb of the right hand into the breech, release a spring, and get the thumb out before the bolt slammed home. When the platoon executed this command correctly there was a loud "CACHUNG" sound of metal on metal as seventy-six bolts clanged home, and it was a wonderful sound. Sooner or later the sliding bolt would catch the thumb, and it would take a brave recruit to play that game again with any confidence. This happened to me one night while drilling. Sergeant Generosity would circle the platoon, repeating the command, "Inspection arms" while trying to locate the guilty late receiver. He finally got to me and he knew what the trouble had to be: the infamous M-1 thumb. He knew I could execute unless my thumb was injured. He didn't say a word, and we marched to our quarters and were dismissed.

We were in competition with two other platoons and were graded on the success of our week's activities. The results were posted so we could keep track of the competition with the winning platoon carrying a special flag the last week of boot camp.

We had our first formal inspection by officers after the second week of our training. Sergeant Generosity thought it would be a good idea for us to run around the grinder as a tune-up for the inspection. Several of us were in condition to sprint the last 100 yards to be among the first to finish. We stood at attention for the better part of an hour, and when we were to march off, our leg muscles had stiffened so that we could barely move let alone march. This inspection was the first chance one poor fellow had to get things off his chest to someone who would listen. He wept as he blubbered the indignities he had to endure. It must have been a sad tale. I ran into him a year or so later, and he had been assigned to a supply depot giving orders like a career marine. He must have straightened things out pretty well for the rest of boot camp!

Our platoon was moved to Camp Matthews, where we would spend three weeks of intensive training to learn to fire the M-1 rifle. Two weeks would be devoted to dry firing (no ammunition), learning the techniques required to becoming proficient with the basic weapon. We had to learn to fire from five basic positions: standing offhand, sitting, kneeling, prone slow fire, and prone rapid fire. We all dreaded the exercise at the prone position, where the left arm supported the weapon with the elbow acting as the base. The rifle coach would come down the firing line, place his toe against the elbow, then grab the barrel of the rifle at the end and pull it toward him until the barrel end touched the ground. You could hear him coming down the line by the protesting sounds of the recruit being administered to. Strangely enough, this exercise was helpful in holding the weapon on the target.

The third week involved live ammunition with four days of firing culminating in firing for record on the fifth day. This determined your status: a no show, marksman, sharpshooter, or expert. On each of the first four days, ten shots were recorded on targets ranging from a 10-inch bull's-eye at 200 yards offhand (standing); a 20-inch bull's-eye prone at 500 yards; a 20-inch bull's-eye at 300 yards, sitting and kneeling; a shoulder silhouette at 200 yards, rapid fire prone; and a shoulder silhouette at 300 yards, rapid fire prone. A shot in the primary target was worth five points so a perfect score for the five positions would be 250 points. If you missed the target altogether, that was a Maggie's drawers, an embarrassing metaphor to any straight-shooting marine.

Any bullet hole on the target could be worth one, two, three, four, or five scores depending on where it struck. The aiming point for the rifle-man was the bottom of the bull's-eye appearing to rest on the forward sight. The idea was to get a group of shots closely bunched so that a sight adjustment of the rear sight would move the next day's group closer to the center of the bull's-eye. The worst thing that could happen was to have ten shots scattered all over the target. The rifle coach was really tough on that pattern, because it was obvious the recruit was not holding his aiming point, and there was no way to help him improve. The sight on the M-1 was adjustable, so if the group was tight, a change in the sight could bring you closer to the center of the target. We recorded our day's firing in our own scorebook. This record would be a help for the next day's shooting.

Each day there would be ten of us at each firing position. On Wednesday the fellow in front of me was verbally addressed for his shot pattern at 200 yards rapid fire; there were no markers close enough to each other to identify a group. The rifle coach turned to me and said he didn't want to see any "blankety blank" group like that out of me. I had 30 seconds to fire ten rounds by simply squeezing the trigger three times, inserting a full clip of seven rounds into the chamber, and squeezing the trigger seven more times. Target 55 disappeared and came back up in a few minutes. There were just two markers in the target; one just under the shoulder silhouette and the other in the silhouette.

There were eight missing markers, and my coach wanted to know what happened. I said I thought I had shot pretty well. We looked at the targets next to us thinking I might have got off on the wrong one. Nothing appeared out of order so the coach got on the phone and called down to the target. He came back in a few minutes and said for me to give him my shooting book. He marked one X out of the bull and nine inside. The one marker covered all nine X's. He didn't have to say anything, but marking my book was high praise from a rifle coach. I guess this shows what one can do when "under the gun."

That day I fired a 231 total, which was only four marks from the boot record. It was the best I would do for circumstances the following days made a good score a long shot. Friday came and it was very foggy. One thousand recruits attempted to certify and only forty earned 190 or better. I had a 210, which was sharpshooter. All the scores were thrown out, and we came back the next day to try again. It was cold and rainy, and my first shot at 500 yards was a 2 at the bottom of the target. I had not made such a poor shot all week, and the rifle coach said I either had a cold round or my sight had been bumped. I made a three-click adjustment and the second shot was a 2 at the top of the target. A cold round doesn't have the normal power so it will fall short, and that is what happened. I had been very accurate at this position, but after three bull's-eyes I managed to lose my patience and came up with a 37 to finish the day with a 218 score, two marks short of expert.

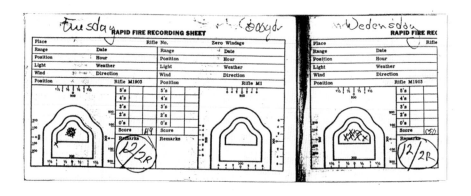

Rapid fire sheet, rifle record card
Horace Hegg, U.S. Marine Corps.

We returned to the Recruit Depot with only a few weeks left in our ten-week training cycle. We were assigned mess duty for the week as part of the training schedule. Sergeant Generosity misread the orders so we reported to Mess Hall 23, which didn't exist. By the time he figured out that we should be at Mess Halls 2 and 3, the Sunday evening meal had been served and cleanup had been completed. The cook for number 3 said he would tell the morning cook that we would need help to learn the routine since we had missed working with the retiring platoon. I was in charge of Mess Hall 3, and things went well through the serving part of the breakfast. Once cleanup started things began to lag.

Cleanup was not going fast enough for the morning cook, even though my troops were running back and forth in the mess hall. He wanted to know who was in charge, and he came to me with the order to get my men on task and to get the lead out—a swift kick in my direction as the punctuation mark. Since he had not asked what our problem was, it was not likely he would listen to any excuse and none was offered. Somehow word finally got to the cook, who called us around him and apologized for not being told of our dilemma. Things rapidly improved, and our mess hall experience finished with record high credits.

The day's routine called for showers before lights out. The head (bathroom) could accommodate about half of our platoon at any one time. The trick was to remove the dungaree pants and shorts, get into the shower, get back into the clothes and boots, run to the Quonset hut, and change into fresh "skivvies" before lights out. I was in the process of unbuttoning when someone called, "Attention!" Several marine officers filed into our quarters as my clothing slid to my ankles. The captain looked me right in the eye for about ten seconds, didn't ask me a single question, then proceeded to the next boot and on down the line. I just stood there the whole time.

One night as I was about to call lights out, two sergeants stepped through the door. One of them looked at me and motioned for me to come outside. I didn't like the looks of this, as there were always rumors about some boot being harassed a bit. I got out the door, and there was the Officer of the Day. He wanted to know what these two sergeants were doing in a restricted area. I recognized Chester Van De Weerd from my hometown and was able to assure the Officer of the Day that they had just come to pay me a little visit. That turned out pretty well, and I appreciated Chester coming around to see me.

One Sunday afternoon several of us were sitting on our locker boxes by our bunks when the rifles started swaying in cadence. We were experiencing an earthquake, but it didn't last very long. We had to look around the area to see if there was any damage. This brought several of us to the "head" where we observed that all the seats had fallen from their normal upright position. All except one, because this boot was using the toilet bowl with the seat still in the upright position. When I asked him why he was sitting on the bowl, he said he thought those things were backrests.

Sergeant Generosity announced that we would be going to a movie on Saturday night. It would be an academy award picture and all the recruits on the base were going to attend. We were looking forward to this event; we had been isolated from the outside world for nine weeks. The title of the picture flashed across the screen; it was Arthur Miller's *Death of a Salesman* with Fredrick March playing the lead role. There was not a sound from the ten thousand troops during the entire performance. We left the theater feeling lower than a duck's belly—so much for a morale booster for the troops.

The training cycle was soon completed, and we were on our way home for a ten-day leave. Mother met me at the bus station in Le Mars, and I could tell by the look on her face that she was a bit disappointed in my appearance. I was wearing the forest green dress uniform, and she was expecting a marine in the white cap and dress blues with the red stripe down the trouser legs. I told Mom that I could wear that uniform if I wanted to spend $150.

My orders were to report back to the field radio school at the Marine Recruit Depot in San Diego by 7:00 A.M. on a certain date. I was to fly directly from Kansas City to San Diego but was rerouted through Los Angeles International and then to San Diego for the same price. This would have made me late reporting for duty, so I had to take a bus from Los Angeles to San Diego. I arrived at the doorstep of the headquarters' office with fifteen minutes to spare. I sat out on the curb until seven o'clock, then went in to hear the duty officer say, "It looks like we got an AWOL (Absent Without Leave)." He said I didn't have to wait until the last minute to report.

I still had the ticket to fly from Los Angeles to San Diego, which could not be cashed for money, but I could use it anytime I wished. I remembered that Sergeant Generosity had a girlfriend in Los Angeles. Since I had no foreseeable use for this ticket, when I saw him drilling his new platoon, I headed toward the platoon. Sergeant saw me and commanded, "Platoon, halt, left face, at ease." He turned to me and asked how I was doing. We visited in whispers when he said aloud, "Why are we whispering? They're not supposed to listen." He was pleased when I offered him the plane ticket; it was the last time I would see him.

Rich Overholtzer had become an ensign in the navy and was stationed on an aircraft carrier docked in San Diego harbor. He had two friends in the area from his hometown, Ida Grove, Iowa: Ron Anderson, in the marines, and Phil Crom, a sales manager for American Tobacco in Southern California. Phil shared an apartment with two others on Mission Beach, and it became a welcome change for us to spend the weekend at the apartment. Phil, who had served in the navy, was on the road all week so was almost like a visitor in his own neighborhood. He seemed to enjoy the three of us dropping in, which we did regularly. We played tennis, golf, and volleyball on the beach and did some surfing. Phil had a new Pontiac convertible and so we were mobile and could get to some interesting tourist attractions. It was pretty glamorous even though nobody knew how to get dates. The convertible was the problem; it would hold only the four of us comfortably.

Phil had learned to cook, so Saturday evening was either a tuna casserole or one of his special meatloaf recipes. Since his two roommates were often gone on the weekend, it was not a hardship for Phil when we stayed over on Saturday evening. I could get "liberty" Saturday noon, take the city bus to Mission Beach, and return to the base Sunday evening.

Liberty was not an automatic thing. We had inspections on Saturday mornings, and if the barracks didn't pass, liberty could be denied for some. We were in the middle of a row of Quonset huts, and the two inspecting officers, on one particular Saturday, started one at each end. We knew that one of the officers routinely found fault with individuals and would deny them liberty. The other was a much easier inspector. We could tell that they would both arrive at our Quonset at the same time. Each inspected his side of the aisle. The strict officer would check a bunk, and if it were not drum tight, he would pull the mattress off the bunk and say to get it right. I was on the other side of the aisle so I could watch the inspection proceed. He came to a clothes locker and turned the handle. About ten wrinkled dress shirts sprung out of that locker. One marine had somehow managed to get through boot camp and into radio school without attracting any great attention to himself, but he never got the hang of sending his shirts to the laundry. He would just go out and buy a new shirt when he had to have a clean one for inspection. The officer was so occupied with this breech of regulations that he could go no further and the rest of the troops were granted liberty for the weekend. The sixteen-year-old, whose true age finally came out, was sent back to civilian life.

After graduation from the field radio school, I was assigned to a communications company, the Third Marine Division, stationed in Camp Pendleton, California. Our company held role call at 8:00 each morning. The sergeant would call out first and last names. I would hear Horace "Haighgh," and I would shout, "Here." It sounded like an echo, and the sergeant would pause and look about. A couple of names later, I would hear him shout Horace "Hegggg," and I would have to answer, "Here," again. The sergeant would give a puzzled look in my direction. This happened a couple of days in a row before I realized that there must be someone in the Marine Corps named Horace besides me. Sure enough, but this guy went by the nickname Chuck Haig. Who would have thought this possible?

Camp Pendleton was the largest military base in the country. It extended up the coast for twenty-five miles and inland about the same. Several marine battalions were scattered throughout the 600 square miles. The land, rugged hills covered with brush, was not suitable for farming. It was a perfect place for a military base. Our company trained daily. As a field radio operator, I grew proficient in the use of several types of radios, from handsets to hand-generated long-range setups.

Our area was self-sufficient in terms of everyday amenities. There was a Post Exchange, an outdoor theatre, a mess hall, and outdoor sports facilities. The schedule usually ended at 4:00 P.M., and overnight liberty was available until 7:00 A.M. the following day. The married marines lived off the base, so it was easy to get a ride to Oceanside if you didn't want to wait for the base bus.

Marines were being sent from the Third Division to the First Division in Korea on a replacement draft. I was expecting to go in early January 1952, when, to my surprise, I appeared on a roster as part of a combat battalion team headed for training in Hawaii. Several hundred marines were soon on our way aboard a transport with several days at sea. We had a pleasant trip and spent time hanging on the rail watching the flying fish.

I saw an ensign on the forward deck discussing a sailor's work with him. I recognized him as a former fellow underclassman at Grinnell. When he had finished, I tapped him on the shoulder to say hello. He recognized me and seemed delighted that I would take the time to visit. The status of the upperclassman took precedence over any rank in this instance. The marines standing around watching this scenario must have wondered what circumstance created that discussion.

We arrived at Pearl Harbor and were transported to the marine air base at Kaneohe on the windward side of Oahu. The captain in charge of our communications company announced that he didn't want us to know the sergeant major of the battalion—either socially or professionally—as this could mean big trouble. Sergeant Stitley had a reputation for being one tough marine. I felt that I could manage this bit of information, and at the first opportunity, found myself at the base golf course, where I proceeded to spend most of my reserve funds on a set of used golf clubs.

We would be at Kaneohe for at least four months, and I was going to make the most of it. As soon as I got on the course, I caught up with two guys in golf shorts. They asked if I would like to join them as they were just learning to play. We introduced ourselves. It was the sergeant major and one of his buddies, First Sergeant Smith of C Company. They had a lot of questions about golf, and when we finished, they asked if I would play with them every day. I said that would be fine. I was taking a liking to them, and they told of many interesting experiences, having been stationed at Kaneohe when it was under attack on December 7, 1941.

Late one afternoon, the three of us went golfing. The course was near the ocean, and some of the tee areas were located on the sand dunes. As we climbed to the top of one of the dunes, I spotted what appeared to be human bones scattered in the sand. The sergeant major said the casualties from the air attack were hastily buried in a large pit near this spot. There was a real fear of an invasion at any moment. Whether these casualties were civilian or military was not determined, and these fragments may have been recovered at some later date.

Sergeant Stitley came into the barracks one afternoon as we were preparing for a conditioning hike with full pack. "Where is Corporal

Hegg?" he asked. "I entered you in the base golf tournament so get over to the golf course right away." The staff sergeant in charge of the hike was not friendly ever since I had guarded him in a pickup basketball game back at Camp Pendleton. He had tried to put me on mess duty on board ship, but I was able to get out of this unpleasant duty because I had recently served a turn at Pendleton. This time he arranged for me to serve a week of mess duty out of rotation, and it was too late to get it straightened out. I reported to the mess hall and the head cook said to come in the next morning.

I got to the golf course and mentioned to Sergeant Stitley that I wouldn't be available for a week. He was surprised that corporals pulled mess duty, and when he found out who was responsible, he said, "That was the guy who was always sitting on the rail of the pool table at the non-commissioned officers club. I'm going to have a little talk with him."

The marines who went on liberty to Honolulu and Waikiki Beach were lucky because we could leave the base in civilian attire. This kept the military police concentrating on uniformed servicemen who were off ship and passing through. One afternoon I recognized a young woman checking IDs at a bar on Waikiki. It turned out to be a classmate from Grinnell College who was spending a year in Hawaii. I mentioned that I would be going to the main island in a few weeks and would be there for two months. She was going to write "Koz" Motobu in Hilo to tell him about my coming there. She forgot to say that I was a marine, and so he went down to the docks in Hilo for three days straight asking sailors if they knew "Ace" Hegg. Koz was a classmate and had played on a volleyball team with me at Grinnell. We eventually got together, and he and his wife gave me a tour of the island that included the Kilauea Crater, which erupted just two years later. I was their guest for dinner, along with another Grinnell classmate, Johnny Ushijima. We caught up on the college days.

Our trip to the big island ended with a tragic event. As an advance party for the battalion, we were to set up a semi-permanent base on the lava fields between the two large volcanoes, Moana Kea and Moana Loa. Our platoon was to set up the communications system for the base. We traveled aboard an LST, and, because it was an overnight journey, we had to bunk in the available space. The acronym LST stood for landing, ship, tank. There were huge doors on the bow that opened like a clam to let the tanks and trucks drive onto the beach during a marine assault landing.

Don Wrage and I set up cots on deck, but the rest of our platoon bunked down in the forward hold in a space in front of some bulldozers. A squall hit during the night and the ship rolled enough to break the chains holding the heavy equipment; three corpsmen were crushed as they lay sleeping. Our men were able to scramble to safety, but it was a very sad day for all of us.

Layers of lava rock covered much of the land between the two volcanoes. A road had been carved out between them. Moana Loa appeared to be a very large mound of built-up lava, whereas Moana Kea was more like a mountain; it has a claim as the tallest mountain in the world if one includes its rising from the seafloor. Our camp was situated at the base of Moana Kea, and one Sunday afternoon I decided to climb the mountain. I got to the tree line when I realized I had told no one of my plan. I might have climbed to the top had I known that the peak would be the future home of the Keck Observatory. This powerful telescope provides astronomers from all over the world with information about the universe. I decided that getting as high as the tree line qualified for climbing the world's tallest mountain. I got myself back to camp without breaking a leg.

The battalion arrived late one evening, and the battalion commander got on the telephone at half past five the following morning. He couldn't reach anyone, as our captain had not set up a switchboard watch until 8:00 A.M. The colonel assigned the captain to the switchboard until 8:00 A.M. and then relieved him of further duties. Due to his mistake, the captain was soon headed for the naval hospital on Oahu. One could understand his being depressed, as this mistake would have a negative effect on his military career.

We had been sleeping past reveille with the advanced party and were still on that time schedule when the colonel showed up outside our tent at eight o'clock, requesting a shore party unit to accompany him into the field. Our six-man team was ready in less than two minutes, which had to be a record for getting dressed for duty. I suspect he knew we were sleeping in, but we had lost our leader, so he let it pass. We spent days dragging a bullhorn and assorted radios over the lava fields to simulate a combat exercise. I was glad when we finally boarded ship to get back to California and Camp Pendleton.

There were two ships taking us across the Pacific: a new Landing-Ship-Dock and our AKA transport, which was showing its age. The colonel rewarded the infantry troops by placing them aboard the new ship with him. Those of us on the old AKA would lean on the rail and watch that new round-bottomed ship roll over on its side and then roll back the other way like an enormous teeter-totter.

One morning we had a shipboard inspection, which included weapons. I was issued a .45-caliber pistol and displayed it on the bunk with the rest of my gear. Then I went topside to wait for the inspecting party to give the all clear. Our sleeping area had a guard posted, but ship personnel had access to our compartment on their way to their quarters. When I returned, the pistol was missing. I had to report this matter to Sergeant Stitley, and he said not to worry, and that he would absolve me of any responsibility for the loss. There was a shakedown involving the entire ship, but the pistol was not recovered.

I heard no more about this business until much later. After I had returned to school at the University of Iowa, I received a large folder with documents from several review committees about this weapon loss. The top sheet wanted my statement as to whether or not I would accept responsibility for the loss of the weapon. One of my roommates at Iowa, Chuck Schaffer from Keokuk, who was studying law and had been an officer in the air force during the war, recommended that I categorically deny any responsibility for the loss of the weapon. Losing one's weapon is not taken lightly in the Marine Corps, regardless of the circumstances.

Soon after returning to Camp Pendleton, I boarded a bus for Iowa on a twenty-day leave. Don was also going home on leave so we traveled together. He asked if I knew how I had been selected from the draft to be in the Marine Corps. He told me he had gone out to have a beer with the sergeant who made the selections at the induction center just a week prior to my being inducted. He had asked about the selection procedure. The sergeant said he had to type twelve copies of the list, and so he picked out all the shortest names. Don's last name is Wrage, and I believed him.

On the bus, I sat next to a Chinese woman who lived in Honolulu and was married to a professional football player. I sat across the aisle from her, and we were soon conversing about what it was like living on the islands.

The bus pulled into Las Vegas, and the driver said that we had a half-hour stop, so Don and I headed for the nearest slot machine arena to try our luck. We kept track of the time and headed back to the bus station only to see our bus pull out in the middle of the street. The driver said we were five minutes late getting back. What he hadn't passed along was that we were also ten minutes late getting into Las Vegas. He would have left us, but my new friend, the Chinese woman, said that if he did, she would report him. Several other passengers chimed in their support.

I had been home for several days when the Marine Corps called at midnight and ordered me to report immediately to Camp Pendleton. My folks wondered what I had done to deserve that kind of attention. I got back to the base to the news that the Third Division had a few weeks to get to full strength in order to replace the First Division in Korea under terms of the cease-fire agreement. Practically every marine in the country was called to Camp Pendleton with the idea that the commanding general could always send back those not needed. One of the requirements for going with a division was to have six months or more left on one's service time. I was a week short of this essential and was placed in a casual company at Pendleton to await my discharge into the reserves.

One day, I observed a sight that will not be viewed by many ever again. I was passing by the mess hall only to hear the marching cadence of a marine who knew how to drill troops. Up the street came this company of marines headed for the mess hall, every one a master sergeant, and they were on parade. You would never see so many hash marks swing on the shirt sleeves of those in a marching body as there were that day. Had I had a camera, the picture could have made the cover of *Life* magazine!

I volunteered for duty in the company office as a typist and found that Sergeant Simmons had aspirations for becoming a professional golfer when his enlistment was completed. He ran the office and time passed quickly working for him. The company commander informed us that the one thing he would not tolerate was for anyone to be absent without leave, and that things would be difficult for anyone under those circumstances. I rose to this challenge. I had nine days leave coming and decided to spend some time in Mission Beach, so I made out my leave papers only to change the leave from nine days to eight days. I forgot that I had made this change, so when I looked at my papers on the ninth day, I realized that I was already AWOL.

I was to meet Rich at the golf course, but simply had to leave him standing on the first tee as I hurried back to Pendleton and the company office. I rushed in the door about noon and Sergeant Simmons asked, "Where have YOU been?" I explained what had happened, and he replied that he thought something like that might have happened. Then he said to get into my uniform and get back to the office. I got into my parade forest greens—with shined shoes, as I expected to see the captain about this matter. This took a good hour, so when I got back to the sergeant, he wondered what took me so long and told me to get back to work. The captain came in a few minutes later and gave me a look as though he thought he should have seen me sooner in the day, but he said nothing. Sergeant Simmons had not reported my absence at morning roll call. He could have lost a stripe if this bit of subterfuge had been discovered!

Ensign Richard Overholtzer, former Grinnell College roommate,
at Mission Beach, California

Part 4

Footprints

Gretchen Thompson and Horace Hegg wedding portrait,
June 4, 1955, Leland, Iowa
Left: Gilbert and Clara Thompson. Right: Palma and Lester Hegg

The Gilbert and Clara Thompson family, 1957
L. to R. back row: Alice, Margaret, Herbert, Marcia, Gretchen, Winnifred
Front row: Gilbert, Gerald, Catherine, David, Clara

Back to the University of Iowa

I was out of active duty and headed for the University of Iowa for the second semester. I arrived by bus mid-afternoon the day before registration, enrolled in practice teaching, and was in class at University High the next day. I met daily for the semester with a biology class of thirty students. This was an unusual class of bright students who were good natured about my inexperience as a student teacher.

One snowy afternoon in late February, I was returning to my rooming house when I came upon a car stuck in the deep snow. The driver was busily shifting gears from reverse to low and back to reverse with no success. To further complicate his problem, he was headed up a small grade. I offered to give him a push and got a couple of people passing by to help. I put my teaching materials in the back seat of the car to keep them out of the snow. We began to push and the car started to move slowly until suddenly it was free of the drift and kept going up the hill with me running after it, shouting, "Wait!" My biology textbook, a unit on reproduction, a week of lesson plans, and some interesting class handout materials were disappearing up the hill and out of sight. I was faced with a problem. A skilled teacher under similar circumstances could "wing it" for a day. I was not that skilled and felt that my credibility as a future teacher would be tested as I walked into the classroom the next morning. There on the teacher's desk were all my backseat teaching materials, and the day got a little brighter.

My supervisor was six months pregnant and had previously taught at the college level. It was a lottery pick to see if she would be around at semester's end. I cannot remember the outcome.

I had found housing at a rooming house for students and shared a dormitory arrangement with four musicians. They were usually gone on the weekends playing gigs. This gave me a chance to clean up the kitchen on Saturday, as this chore was routinely neglected. I took all my meals at the Union so I was not involved in creating this little problem.

It wasn't long before I heard that two grad students were looking for a third person to share an upstairs apartment. The story was that this vacancy had occurred when a law school graduate finally gave up his interest in events in the apartment house across the street. He had spotted a newlywed couple living in a second floor apartment. When the bride came home from class, she would be completely undressed by the time she got to the second floor. The third floor apartment gave the fellow an unobstructed view of that apartment. His interest waned when the leaves came out on the trees obstructing the view. John and Chuck swore that this was a true story—it seemed reasonable. I moved in for the remainder of the semester knowing that there would be no verifying that story.

John Pagin was engaged and would be married on the fourth of July in Keokuk, Iowa. Chuck and I would be invited to the wedding, and I would be Chuck's guest. One day John was upset by a package he had received. It was to be Virginia's wedding gift, a beautiful Steuben vase. He had found a poem that he favored and sent it to the Steuben Company with the instruction that the two-stanza poem should be etched on the vase. The vase cost $60 and the etching $240. John said to not tell Virginia; she would never use it if she knew the cost. John was in his early thirties and had come from an old family of some wealth and community stature. He was a product of the old school, and being an officer in the war only solidified his notion of the order of things. His ambition was to teach history in a military or prep school setting.

I was back to work at the Student Union—bussing tables at the evening meal during the week and acting as checker at the cash register on the weekends. We had our regular customers, who were mostly students, while visitors made up the majority on Sunday. One lady ate all of her evening meals at the cafeteria. She may have been a graduate student in her middle forties, and she must have been on a tight budget. She had the same fare almost every night and always paid the cashier with the correct amount of change. She would have her meal and then come back for a cup of coffee, which was eight cents. It was convenient for her to hand me the money, and I would get her coffee.

Sunday noon was a busy time with people standing in line waiting to pay. Chicken potpies in little porcelain dishes were a feature that day. My coffee customer came with her eight cents, and as she reached between two customers waiting in line to pay, the nickel slid out of her grasp and disappeared in another lady's chicken potpie. She looked at me, but she might as well have been looking at Buddha for all the help she would get from me. I was inexplicably—frozen in time. I was in charge of the cafeteria's profits; Scrooge would have been proud. The coffee lady picked up a spoon from the tray and fished out that nickel, wiped it clean with a paper napkin, and handed me the nickel—all observed by the lady who had just paid for the chicken potpie. The lady with the pie gave a little sigh, picked up her tray, and disappeared into the crowd. I made the mistake of telling this event to Gwen, the manager; she gave me a disgusted look and said I should have gotten a new chicken pie for the lady and a free cup of coffee to boot! She was right!

The semester had come to a close, and I had my teaching certificate to teach in the secondary schools in Iowa. I was also on the GI Bill and not in any hurry to go out into the world as a wage earner. Besides, I could work at the Student Union for my meals and school administration seemed to be a direction I should go. I had John's wedding invitation to look forward to, so it was comfortable to stay in summer school. I moved into the Delta Tau Delta fraternity house for the summer. Roger had returned from the marines and was back in school living at the house. There was also a spare room for me.

Rich and Phil were coming to Iowa City for the weekend of the fourth and were happy to hear that I was in summer school. This became a dilemma for me, but I decided John needed my presence at his wedding, so I would miss being with my Ida Grove friends for much of their time on campus. This decision had a huge effect on my future. Rich's younger brother, Bob, who was also in school, arranged dates for Rich, Phil, Roger, and Bruce Snell, another Grinnell classmate from Ida Grove. All the dates were nurses, and the guys got along so well they eventually married the girls they met on this date.

I was in Keokuk for the wedding; it was hot in that church. John looked miserable with the sweat dripping off his nose and little puffs of breath exiting at regular intervals from his pursed lips. Virginia was love-ly and seemingly not bothered by the heat. Soon after the newlyweds were on their way, I returned to Iowa City. A year later John was teaching at a private school in South Bend, Indiana, and my new bride and I would get to see the married couple during a Hawkeye-Notre Dame football weekend at South Bend. I have since lost track of them.

Two Norwegians

July 8, 1954, found me walking to one of my morning classes. Coming toward me was a person who looked familiar. It was Letha Sorenson, a girl I had met through a mutual friend. We had ridden the roller coaster together at Arnold's Park at Lake Okoboji eight years prior.

She recognized me and we exchanged pleasantries, one being that she had just married the past weekend. I mentioned that I was working in the cafeteria at the Union. That afternoon, when I stopped at the River Room at the Student Union, I saw Letha with two other young women. She invited me to join them, and I met Gretchen. We visited for a time, and I learned that Gretchen would be studying at the education library that evening. I had been casually dating Maggie, a student whom I met while working in the cafeteria. Maggie was searching for a spiritual home, having tried Christianity, Judaism, and the Islamic religions. She was studying that evening with her organic chemistry tutor, so after finishing work, I found myself headed for the education library. Sure enough, Gretchen and her sister Margy were studying at one of the tables. They soon went out for some air, and I followed to reintroduce myself. I asked Gretchen if she would be interested in going out for coffee. We headed for downtown just a couple of blocks away.

The Airliner served coffee although it was a beer tavern and a popular hangout for the college students. We spent a good hour getting acquainted; Gretchen knew all about me by the time we were ready to leave. As we were leaving, I spotted Maggie having a beer with her tutor; I waved and she waved back. Gretchen and I walked to Currier Hall, and I asked if I could give her a call. We said goodnight. I saw Maggie the next day and told her about Gretchen. She said, "You ought to marry that girl!" That was the last I would see of Maggie for almost a year.

Gretchen and I had our first date a couple of days later. We saw the movie *The Wild One* with Marlon Brando as the leader of a motorcycle gang. We stopped at the Airliner after the movie, and apparently everyone there had seen the picture. A gentleman strode into the lounge dressed in leather jacket, leather cap, and the boots. As if on cue, arms reached out to an imaginary throttle and we all gunned it!

Gretchen Thompson

Gretchen and I began seeing each other daily, and classes soon became just a formality. She was an elementary school teacher, from a farm background, a Norwegian, and a few months younger than I. She had beautiful brown eyes, and I knew that I wanted to look into them forever. I soon asked her to marry me and she hesitated about ten seconds before saying, "YES!" Our engagement had come about in what some folks might consider a short time—sixteen days—so we decided not to announce our plans until we had obtained a ring.

We planned to be married the following June, and I had to think about getting a teaching position for the coming year. My credentials went to the placement office at the university on a Thursday morning in early August. When I got back to the fraternity house, I had a message from the office that a superintendent was on his way to Iowa City and that I should meet with him at 1:30 that afternoon. Mr. Isenberger offered me the science position at the public school in Hudson, Iowa. I agreed to come to Hudson in a few days to sign a contract.

School was over, and I was back in Rock Valley. Brother Peer had graduated from high school and was enrolled at Luther College for the coming year. I asked him if he had thought about playing basketball at the University of Iowa, and he said he would be interested. I knew Bucky O'Connor, the Iowa basketball coach, and arranged to meet him at a basketball clinic in Ames. Bucky offered Peer a full scholarship on the spot. We continued on to Hudson, where Superintendent Isenberger introduced me to John Wrobleski, who would be my principal.

I rented a room not far from the school from an elderly lady. Mrs.

McMann had been hoping for a male teacher to rent her spare bedroom. She would always invite me for breakfast in the coming school year. Uncle Sherman was the Dodge/Plymouth dealer in Cedar Falls just eight miles north of Hudson. He and Aunt Eleanor were pleased that I would be teaching close by. Lynne, Nancy, and Sigrid rounded out the family, and it would be good to get better acquainted with my young cousins.

Palma had met Gretchen in Iowa City during one of her trips around the state as president of the Iowa Medical Auxiliary. She invited Gretchen to come to our home for a visit before school started. The train pulled into the station, and Gretchen stepped off into my hug. We were happy to be together again.

Dad was very formal around members of the opposite sex; all were addressed as Miss or Mrs. It was no different with Gretchen, but even so you could tell that he knew he was gaining a daughter-in-law. Mother was thrilled, especially because she had only brothers and sons in her family; she set a high place for Gretchen.

Gretchen's farm home, Leland, Iowa
The house was built over the original log cabin.

Science Teacher

I got to Cedar Falls a few days later and borrowed a car from Uncle Sherm until I could buy one from him. I soon bought a new 1954 Plymouth Savoy and had to pick it up from the dealer in Independence, Iowa. The car was fully serviced and ready to go when we arrived to pick it up. Cousin Lynne rode the thirty miles back to Cedar Falls with me. Halfway there, the engine began making a screeching sound and the car began to shudder. This was very upsetting, but it soon stopped making the noise. When I explained this to Uncle Sherm, he said not to worry; the engine was probably a little tight. I would call upon him many times about the condition of the car. I got him out of bed one night upon returning from a trip to the farm; I noticed the oil pressure needle dropped down a couple of notches as I sat at a stop sign. He said not to worry.

There were fourteen new faculty members in the high school that fall. It would be a learning situation for all of us as well as the students who had enjoyed a free rein in terms of discipline the preceding year. The first day began, and we had zero tolerance for attitudes. The principal laughed as he recounted the day. Fifteen students had been escorted to his little pigeon-loft office by the last bell of the day. A few moments later another set of heels was heard being dragged up the steps by the seventh grade science teacher. The students got the message, and by the end of the week things had settled down and learning was in progress. As a teacher, the students you taught in your first year are remembered. Most of them would still address me as Mr. Hegg, and that is always a nice surprise.

Saturday morning arrived, and I was to meet Gretchen in Humboldt, Iowa, where she and her sister Margy were elementary school teachers. We would continue to the farm, where I would meet Gilbert and Clara Thompson, my future in-laws. Uncle Sherm's Doberman had a litter of pups that needed a home. I thought it would be a nice gesture to bring one of those pups to the farm, as they had no dog on the place. I fixed a box on the floor in the front seat, and that pup barked all the one hundred miles to Humboldt.

Gretchen and Margy wanted to do some shopping in Fort Dodge twenty miles south of Humboldt. It was so hot that we thought it best to leave the pup at the fire station to entertain the firemen while we went shopping. When it came time for supper, we stopped at a little roadside restaurant on the outskirts of town. It had cooled down enough so that it was safe to leave the pup in the car in the uncovered box while we were inside. On returning to the new car, I could see the pup had climbed out of the box and up onto the rear window shelf. Opening the door was not a pleasant experience. "Uffda!" Some paper towels got us back to traveling shape, but the dog picked up the name Uffda, which in Norwegian means "dumb."

Gilbert and Clara made me feel welcome, and I was pleased to remember what my dad had told me, "If you want to know what a young woman would be like when she is older, just look to her mother." Clara was a comfort, and, as I soon learned, equalled by few. Gilbert was the personification of the family farmer. He worked with a patient intelligence that provided for nine children, who were all important contributors to life's stream. Gilbert would faithfully keep a record of each day that he lived. He would laugh from time to time about the silly town pup trying to make it on the farm.

The State Teachers' Convention was in early November in Des Moines. We made a quick check of the exhibits, and then headed for Plumb's to select an engagement ring. The gentleman ushered us into a private room and brought out a tray of diamonds for us to study. He went over the merits of each stone, and then we had to decide. One in particular seemed to be just right. He recommended a setting of a single diamond and would send it to me at Hudson as soon as it was ready. Within the week, I had the ring and set out for Humboldt as soon as school was out. It was a perfect way to announce our engagement.

The school year went by with weekly trips to Humboldt and the farm. Plans were made for a June 4 wedding at the Lutheran church in Leland. My folks arranged an engagement reception for us to be held at the Sheldon golf clubhouse in the spring. Many friends from Rock Valley were there to wish us well. Relatives came from as far away as Madison, Wisconsin.

The Newlyweds

The wedding day arrived, and Bill Rozeboom had flown in from Cleveland. Brother Peer was to be best man, and Gretchen's sister Margy was to be the bridesmaid. Eric Guiere, a tenor and friend of Margy's, came from Minneapolis to provide the solo music. Maurice Anderson, a Humboldt friend, came from Albert Lea to be the organist. The reception was held in the church basement, and the place was packed with local friends, relatives, and a number of Rock Valley friends. Wayne Stark and his wife came from Hudson. Wayne was the proprietor of the Blue Goose restaurant in Hudson, where I had taken many of my evening meals.

Gretchen's cousin Chris recognized Dad as someone who had stopped at his farm to buy gas early one morning. He said that Dad had given him a ten-dollar tip for the gas, which he said was the biggest tip he had received from passing motorists. Dad was on his way to Harmony, Minnesota, to see his mother that day.

A photo taken as we were leaving the altar found me looking down at the floor as if I were looking for a place to take the next step. Gretchen, a beautiful bride, radiated confidence in her smile.

We were soon on our honeymoon, and I can recall driving five miles under the speed limit as we headed to Lutsens, a resort on the north shore of Lake Superior in Minnesota. The weather was typically cold and rainy for early June. We shared the resort with four busloads of high school seniors, which made me think twice about sponsoring senior trips.

One of the things you do when in Minnesota is fish. I had never had much luck as a fisherman but with my newlywed status, I thought my luck would be better. I rented a boat, some fishing gear, and bought some bait. With Gretchen aboard, I rowed out to what seemed like a good spot and was about to fish when I realized that I had not purchased a license. So back we went and, ten dollars poorer, started out once again. We sat for two hours and not a bite.

We returned to the farm and packed for the trip to Iowa City, where I would be going to school for the summer. I had rented an apartment, and, within two blocks of the place, a car tooted at us from a side street as we passed through the intersection. I pulled over and got out to see what the toot was about. It was Maggie with her new husband. We laughed and listened and went on our ways. Our paths would not cross again.

Our first home was a downstairs apartment in an old two-story white house with a big front porch. There was a living room, a small kitchen, and a bathroom with a shower stall. There was a hide-a-bed sofa in the living room, which we converted each evening. It was new, but we still rolled to the middle. It was a hot summer with no air-conditioning.

Going to the movies was our chief source of entertainment. Television was just becoming a feature in daily life, but we would wait until our home in Hudson to add this to our lives.

We had Roger Anderson and Jerry Nordquist as dinner guests one evening and Gretchen was up to the task. We used a card table, three electric fry pans, four-place pottery ware, and stainless flatware—all wedding gifts in use for a memorable time. I don't remember what we ate, but our guests were lavish in their praise.

I had rented an upstairs apartment in Hudson. The outside steps leading to it were rather steep, and the last step was not uniform with the rest. It would not pass a building code today, but there wasn't such a code in Hudson in the fall of 1955. Anyway, we were newlyweds and thought we were immortal; somehow no mishap occurred. Our landlords eventually rebuilt the steps. They said they would sleep better having corrected the stair problem.

Family Additions

October came and the news was that we were expecting our first child, due the middle of April. Philip Raymond Hegg was born on April 11, 1956. He was so strong that he lifted his head right up off the baby mattress while still in the hospital nursery. Dr. Richard Miller said Philip could get right up and walk off the delivery table.

Dad and Mom came over from Rock Valley. They would go the three hundred miles back the same day, so we headed right to the hospital. I said that visiting hours were at eleven, but Dad had on his doctor look, and we breezed by the front desk and the nurse's station to view baby Philip. I don't know what there is about this custom, especially when one has delivered over a thousand babies, but Dad seemed properly impressed that he now had a grandson.

Gretchen's mom would come down to stay for several days as we recuperated. I had been up most of the night that Philip was born but was able to get to school that day. I dozed off for a second right in the middle of giving an assignment. The class got a big kick out of that.

A year went by and we got a call from a Harry Green, a farmer who had built a house in Hudson only to find his son's army commitment was extended. This meant that Harry would have to stay on the farm for another year, and he would have to rent out the new house in town. He asked if we were interested in renting the *House Beautiful* 1953 Home of the Year for Brides. The magazine gave an entire issue to featuring this house.

Harry was a U.S. Steel farm-building salesman, and he had seen this model featured in a home show in Iowa City. He came home to Hudson, purchased a lot in town, and called the U.S. Steel Company to send out the model home. U.S. Steel had not planned to distribute this building west of the Mississippi, but he was persuasive and so the pre-fab was delivered. Harry and his wife had gone to Fredrick's Furniture in Grundy Center and bought new furniture to completely furnish the house. He would rent it to us for the sum of one hundred dollars a month with the caveat that the natural gas furnace being installed would not be available until early in the fall; there was no heat in the building in the meantime.

My take-home pay was two hundred fifty-three dollars a month, but we took the offer. Our electric bill was over fifty dollars the first month, and it was November before the natural gas was hooked up. Harry gave us a goose, two roasting hens, and a fifty-dollar reduction in the rent as a Christmas present that December.

George and Jeanne Strayer had invited us to their home for dinner before Philip was born. I saw Harry's gift as a chance to invite them to dinner. Jeanne was the daughter of Mrs. McMann. I had become acquainted with them during my bachelor year at Hudson. George was the executive officer of *The Soybean Digest*, headquartered in Hudson. He had been offered a position as the head of the Department of Agriculture in the Eisenhower administration and had turned it down. They were world travelers. making several trips to Japan promoting soybean products.

The two roasting hens seemed the right fare for an elegant dinner. We sat at the small dining area, and Gretchen brought out the two roasted hens. I was to carve them. When I thrust the fork into one of the carcasses, it spun right off the table onto the floor. George and Jeanne were very gracious and didn't laugh until they got home.

Summer came, and I began selling life insurance as a part-time job. We moved into a downstairs apartment the following year, and Sara Elizabeth Hegg was born June 19, 1959. After teaching at Hudson for four years, I decided to become a full-time life insurance salesman.

We built a house and moved into it on October 5, 1960. Grandpa Gilbert had sold some walnut trees from the woods at the farm and had the large limbs sawed into planks that were drying in the loft of the barn. He offered them to us for our new house, so one wall and the bookcase were done in a random board-and-batten pattern, which has been an important feature in making the house we designed even more unique.

Erika Marie Hegg was born on November 13, 1962, and Christian Theodore Hegg was born January 5, 1964. Our family was now complete. The cycle of new lives had begun.

One could tell early on that Philip was going to be a good athlete someday. When he was four, he could swing a plastic bat and hit a plastic ball nearly every time I would pitch it. This was a golf practice ball, and he would line it right over my head. When he was old enough to play summer baseball, the only time he would get an out was when he left first base too soon. He would usually get picked to play as a substitute on one of the older kids' teams.

The Ford Motor Company started sponsoring Pass, Punt, and Kick Contests throughout the country, and Philip first participated at age eight. He won the local contest and was eligible to compete in Des Moines. We got to Des Moines, and Philip was so confident he would win that he could hardly wait his turn. He punted right over the judge's heads and easily won the state competition for eight-year-olds. His score was the top one in the country that day, and he was invited to the next level of competition to be held in Chicago during half-time of the Bears/Forty-Niners game in Wrigley Field.

Doug Keith, the local Ford dealer, his family, Gretchen, Philip, and I flew to Chicago to be part of this winners' celebration. Sara, Erika, and baby Christian stayed with Frank and Colleen Gardner, who were our best friends in Hudson. Mark, Jan, and Patricia were in the same age group as our children, and they were best of friends, but it was generous of Colleen to take the kids for the weekend.

We left the Waterloo airport in a two-engine DC-3. After arriving in Chicago, we were taken to one of the big hotels in time for Philip to be completely outfitted in a Chicago Bears' uniform. A banquet was held that evening and several of the Bears players were present, including George Halas, the famous coach of the Bears. A satin banner was hanging on the wall for each of the twelve contestants (two from each age group) with the name printed in big letters. Doug had misspelled Philip's name, so it was on the banner like Phillips Petroleum, which was an understandable mistake. His banner was signed by a number of the players and is a fine souvenir of that time.

Philip had grown a very full head of hair by his eighth birthday—maybe because I was his barber—and we had all got used to seeing it long. This was before long hair was popular, and Uncle Sherm thought he was doing us a favor by taking Philip to a real barber and getting him a "butch." This was the same as Sampson having his locks shorn! Philip couldn't even recognize himself when he looked in the mirror. The winner of this contest would go on to compete in the finals in Miami. Luck proved to be the big player in Chicago with the wind blowing and below freezing temperatures. Philip had to lead his squad onto the field through the goal posts and to the nearest hash mark. He had to ask, "What is a hash mark?" I was relieved that we didn't have to go to Miami, and it was a memorable trip to Chicago.

The Horace Hegg family, Christmas 1966
L. to R.: Back: Horace, Philip, Gretchen
Front: Erika, Sara, Christian

I installed a basketball hoop and bang board on the front of the new house, and not a day went by without the kids shooting baskets or playing a pickup game. It didn't matter if it was summer or winter, there would be either a basketball game in the driveway or a football game in the backyard. We lived on a cul-de-sac, which also proved to be a good place for a tennis game as there was little traffic to disrupt the volleys.

The Trip West

We bought a new 1969 Dodge Sportsman van and planned a trip to California to visit Brother Peer and his family, who were living in Hacienda Heights near Los Angeles. The van was an eleven passenger with two bench seats facing each other and a third bench in the rear. It was grass green with a prominent white band through the mid-section. It was a beauty! I removed the rear bench and replaced it with a plywood table supporting a foam mattress. Gretchen sewed curtains for all the windows, and we were ready for the big trip. The area beneath the "bed" would be used to store our personal gear, sleeping bags, and a little Coleman stove. We planned to camp and picnic our way across the nearly two thousand miles to California.

We had two hundred dollars and a gasoline credit card to sustain us. I stopped at the post office as we were leaving, and there was a Mastercard in the box. This was a new idea for us, but we thought it might be useful to have that money backup. It was at least a year before the expenses of that trip were fully paid. The van was designed so the driver sat over the front wheels, and the engine compartment was between the driver and the front seat passenger. There was no protection for anyone in the front seats in the event of a head-on collision. One was supposed to avoid that sort of thing. Christian would stand with his nose practically on the windshield, as he didn't want to miss any of the view. I had rigged a board with a foam mattress that covered the engine compartment nicely. The plan was for Christian to sleep on this if we ever used the van for sleeping.

We started out by mid-morning and planned to get to Lincoln, Nebraska, where we would stay with Gretchen's brother Jerry and his wife, Betty. Jerry was an economics professor at the University of Nebraska. He had been a B-17 pilot with twenty-five missions over Germany. Margaret Bourke White had photographed him on the steps of the Old Capitol at Iowa City, and his picture was on the cover of *Life* magazine, April 17, 1947, featuring the war veteran returning to college.

We set out for Colorado Springs the next day and arrived in the evening. I wanted to visit the Colorado College campus to show the family where I had spent a summer. It was dark and raining, and we were tired from the day's ride. No one was too impressed. We had decided to spend the night in the van and managed to find a trailer court where the manager gave us permission to park on the street. Sara and Erika were to sleep on the foam mattress, Philip underneath on the floor, Gretchen and I would each have a bench seat, and Christian would be on the space over the engine bonnet between the front seats.

Morning came. We traveled halfway up Pike's Peak and had a picnic breakfast at a small park along the side of the road. It was one of the highlights of our trip. We made it to Raton, New Mexico, that day. Christian jumped into the motel pool and swam all the way across the deep end. We didn't even know he could swim. It was on to Cimarron, Taos, New Mexico, and Durango, Colorado, where we camped out for the night.

Mesa Verdi was our first stop the next morning. One tried to visualize how people lived on this rugged plateau over a thousand years ago. We stopped at the Four Corners in early afternoon, so named because Colorado, New Mexico, Arizona, and Nevada share the same location. One can stand in all four states at the same time, and we all took turns at that phenomenon. Late afternoon found us staring out over the Grand Canyon, and we ended the day with a motel stop at Williams, Arizona.

The final day of our journey took us through the Arizona desert. The van lacked air conditioning; we could feel the heat and made a stop for ice. I remarked to the store clerk that it was pretty hot at 104 degrees. He laughed and said it had been 117 degrees the day before. We arrived in Hacienda Heights and Brother Peer's home after five days of travel.

Peer, Patricia, and their children, Laura, Cary, and Lisa, made room for us. The week was devoted to visiting Disneyland, Knott's Berry Farm, Camp Pendleton, Mission Beach, and Gretchen's brother David in Irvine. Peer had become a prominent amateur golfer in Southern California, and I was treated to a couple of rounds of golf at his home course.

We started back taking the northern route through Las Vegas, where we stopped for lunch at Sambo's House of Pancakes. We camped out at Cedar Breaks National Monument near Cedar City, Utah. The next day on to Salt Lake City and Rawlings, Wyoming, where we spent the night in a motel. We drove the last eight hundred miles, and we were back in Hudson having traveled over four thousand miles. The kids were great travelers, but it was good to be home again.

Closing the Circle

The legendary freehand circle, November 1968
West Intermediate School, Waterloo, Iowa

My interest in selling life insurance had waned and the prospects for a career in finance had not materialized. I returned to teaching in the Waterloo schools and retired in 1993. I coached basketball, wrestling, golf, girl's basketball, softball, and volleyball.

If a single moment in my teaching experience could be singled out as a memorable event, it was the day I was teaching fractions to a ninth grade class in Special Education. Two students were on the verge of getting the concept of a fraction. I went to the blackboard to draw a picture of a pie to show how it could be divided into pieces, each piece being a fraction of the whole. With a swing of the arm, I had produced what could be called a perfect freehand circle. Dr. Gale, my physics professor at Grinnell College, was proud of his ability to draw a freehand circle but nothing like this. It was centered on a clean blackboard, the line was pure, and there was no noticeable beginning or ending. It was not symmetrical and yet it was visually perfect. There was no more talk of fractions that day.

The math teacher next door had to get a meter stick to see if it met her definition of perfect. The orchestra leader climbed three flights of stairs to view this phenomenon, and after looking at it, he had to be restrained from erasing what he thought was a hoax. The circle remained on that board for over a year. Students who had been in class that memorable day stopped by from time to time to see that circle! I left my room after school one day and when I came back, the circle had disappeared. A substitute janitor had missed the word "save" when he cleaned the boards.

End of an Era

In the later years of Dad's morning routine, he would take the time to stop at the local restaurant for morning coffee and visit with the regular customers over the day's news. He would park into the curb, and if he was running a bit late, would back out against traffic to take a shortcut to the office. One day he stopped in the law office of Tom McGill, a classmate, tossed a traffic ticket on the desk, and asked Tom to take care of it and send him the bill. Two highway patrolmen were in town and were not impressed with Dad's interpretation of the law. Tom said that when he looked at the ticket, there was more than just a simple fine.

Dad had not been wearing his glasses and was subject to an automatic suspension of his driver's license. Tom made a call to the state patrol and the solution was for Dad to go sixty miles to Spencer and take a written test. "No, this will not do; I'll retire first!" Tom called and the site was moved to Rock Rapids. Still, "No!" He called Orange City and the response was the same. Finally Tom called the headquarters in Boone and said, "If you can't come up with a solution to this problem, there will be carloads of protesters tooting their horns all the way to patrol headquarters." It was arranged that the two patrolmen should come to the office and give the test. They sat waiting their turn, went in, and asked one question. They stopped at Tom's office and said, "He passed."

There was one time of the year when it got extra busy in Dr. Hegg's home and that was income tax time. For several years he had done his own tax preparation, and it was usually the last day for filing. Brother Peer tells me Dad eventually hired Earl Gort in the bank to do all this for him. The one stipulation was that the Iowa return should not be submitted until the day before it was due. One day he received a late notice from the state and tossed it on Earl's desk for him to pay the penalty. The amount was less than seventy-five dollars, but it was not a trivial amount, either. Earl paid the penalty, and in a few weeks went to Dr. Hegg to pay his bill for delivery of their new baby. He was told to sign a blank check, and it would be filled out later. Earl did just that and waited for the check to clear the bank. It was made out for three dollars, the price of an office call.

Dad and Mom's fortieth wedding anniversary arrived, and friends in

Rock Valley made this a special occasion. Hundreds of cards from friends and former patients were part of the celebration. It would be their last wedding anniversary.

A new hospital was in the process of being built, and it would be named Hegg Memorial Hospital. Dad gave his permission with the admonition that the name would be appropriate by the time it was completed.

Dr. Hegg died May 7, 1967, three months before the hospital was completed. A few days before his death, he told me he thought that he had given his community a good medical practice. I could only nod my agreement.

Our family traveled across the state from Hudson to Rock Valley on the Sunday morning of his death; the sky was black and the wind howled. The funeral service was held in the Dutch Reform Church, which was the largest in town. Eight hundred friends were the congregation and one could hear the silence. Our family left for the farm that afternoon, and as we pulled onto the highway, the hearse came up a side road ahead of us, headed for a second service the following day in Harmony, Minnesota. It was a melancholy moment—the end of an era.

After that service and committal in Harmony, friends and relatives were invited to a dinner at the banquet room of the local restaurant. As I moved past a row of booths on my way to the dining room, an elderly man waved to me from one of them and asked, "Are you a son of Lester?' He was the man who had been haying with Lester the day he announced he was going to become a doctor. I was too caught up in the day to get the gentleman's name and to invite him to the dinner to share that precious moment.

Les had always called Mother "Polly," and he had left her with sufficient funds to live comfortably. She had learned to be a helping partner in his practice, and at the same time, she had developed a lifestyle that enabled her to proceed on her own terms. She traveled to Norway and was there when the "Astronauts" landed on the moon; she had become even more of a celebrity. She was fond of flying, and nothing could deter her feeling for adventure. We were to meet her at the airport in Waterloo one February day. The weather was near-blizzard conditions, and I questioned that the plane would even land. Suddenly headlights from a plane appeared, and it taxied onto the apron a good fifty yards from the gate. I thought surely an attendant would help an elderly person from the plane to the gate. Here came Polly down the ramp with the wind blowing and the snow flying. She made it to the gate before I could get out to help. She was laughing at the whole experience.

Polly spent a few days with us, and then it was time for her to return home to Rock Valley. She took the bus from Cedar Falls—eight miles north of Hudson—and had arranged for friends to meet her at the bus depot in LeMars, Iowa, just thirty miles south of Rock Valley. Mother counted all the towns along the way and figured there would be eleven stops. As she told the story, she hadn't realized the bus would also stop in Remsen, which was several miles off the direct line to LeMars. It was a Sunday evening and the temperature was 20 below zero. The eleventh stop came, and she got off the bus. The town was deserted, and she realized her mistake in time to catch two nuns who had been on the bus and were about to drive away. They listened to her story and were able to drive her to LeMars in time to catch her friends, who were having coffee at the bus depot while trying to figure out what had happened to Polly.

She moved to Cedar Falls to be near us in June 1986; many of her friends back in Rock Valley were dying. She was a part of our family for the ten years left in her life. She died quietly on October 25, 1996, at age ninety-three. A stone in Greenhill Cemetery in Harmony, Minnesota, marks the remains of Lester and Palma Hegg.

Palma Hegg, center, is received by Ambassador and Mrs. Val Peterson at the American Embassy residence, Helsinki, Finland.

Dr. Lester Hegg's office, Rock Valley, Iowa

Sioux Center Hospital nursing staff who worked with Dr. Lester Hegg
L. to R.: Mrs. Wanda Punt, Mrs. Esther Biemers, Mrs. Eva Dykstra,
Mrs. Karen Boer, Miss Willy Dekker, Mrs. Roberta Calon (seated)

Hegg Memorial Health Center
Rock Valley, Iowa

The Hegg Memorial Hospital was dedicated in 1967. A doctors' clinic and nursing home were added later, including a cardiac rehabilitation unit and wellness center. The complex is known today as the Hegg Memorial Health Center.

More Family Memories

Visiting the Thompson farm was one of the highlights for our family. Gilbert and Clara seemed pleased that the children looked forward to this adventure. Gilbert would sit in his big leather rocking chair with one or more of his grandchildren on his lap reading them a story. It would remind him of some event from the past, and then he would finish telling the event with a deep, slow chuckle that put an end to it. Clara would be in the kitchen fixing something good to eat. Clara would get out to the barn and even help with the milking, they tell me. She didn't drive the car, but she could get out on the tractor if the need would arise.

Clara always had a big garden that included a strawberry patch, potatoes, tomatoes, beans, and the root crops. She had flowers for the table, and offshoots of her heirloom peonies are growing today at our home. Gilbert maintained an orchard with ten different varieties of apples; a grapevine covered with beta grapes grew on the windmill tower. Clara would send something in season from the garden with us. There were forty acres of woods as part of the one hundred twenty acres that was the Thompson farm. The Winnebago River flowed on the western edge of the woods, and there was fishing for the children. Gilbert ranged his cattle in the woods, so the ground cover was short and made for easy access to this quiet place. Bluebells, trillium, sweet William, and wild roses were in abundance during their season. One could find an occasional jack-in-the-pulpit growing in a hidden sanctuary; the trees in the woods were black oak, walnut, wild plum, and basswood. Gretchen's youngest brother, David, was an outdoorsman, and he would supply the table with pheasant or wild duck on occasion. He became an aeronautical engineer and helped design space equipment used in the Mars space landing. He and sister Marcia are co-owners of the farm—preserving its history as a Century Farm in Iowa farm lore. Over the years, the nine brothers and sisters have gathered at the farm for a day of reminiscing and to get acquainted with the newest additions. October 11, Clara's birthday anniversary, has become the traditional time for this "get-to-gather."

Gilbert passed away November 25, 1968, at age seventy-eight. Clara lived to be ninety-three and died of natural causes March 30, 1989. The remains are marked in the Leland Cemetery intermingled among the oaks on a hill overlooking the Winnebago River.

Our Athletic Children

Our four children were all prominent athletes in their high school and college careers. Philip was a highly regarded All-State quarterback in high school and was recruited by the University of Iowa, where he had a good career as a tight end and wide receiver.

I got home from school one day in time to see the fourth quarter of Christian's junior high game with NU Junior High. The score was 6-0 in favor of the visitors. Christian was playing right defensive end; they swept around his end and went for a touchdown, making the score 12-0. At the supper table that evening, I asked Christian how they scored the first touchdown. He said, "They went around my end in the first half, too."

Christian was the first-team All-State Elite quarterback his senior year in high school. He played on three state-qualifying football teams and one state-qualifying basketball team. Following in his brother Philip's footsteps, he was chosen to the North squad of the Dr. Pepper basketball camp and was the starting quarterback for the North team in the Shrine game. He accepted a full scholarship at the University of Northern Iowa. He played at Independence Junior College his sophomore year and transferred to Northeast Missouri State for his junior and senior years. He was voted Player of the Year by conference coaches his senior year. In recognition of his fine year, no other nominees were considered by the conference coaches. He was elected to first team quarterback All-American, College Division, by the Associated Press and the Football Coaches Association for his play at Northeast, now renamed Truman University.

The game with Central State of Ohio is remembered as one of the most important and most exciting in the school's history. The nation's leading defense and second-leading offense were pitted against Northeast's nation-leading offense in Division 2. After trailing 24-0 in the first quarter, Northeast won the game in the final minute 46-45. Chris threw for five touchdowns in the come-from-behind win.

Chris was elected to the Truman University Hall of Fame and was chosen as one of three quarterbacks on the All-Century squad during the twentieth century of football at Northeast Missouri State.

Sara was a four-year starter in basketball and softball at Hudson, earning All-Conference honors in both sports. She was a catcher for her first year in softball and put out three base runners at home plate in the sectional tournament, although they lost to the second-ranked team in the state. She switched to shortstop and continued to make big plays in both softball and six-person basketball as a forward. Sara earned her master's degree at UNI and is still fielding the hard grounders as principal of Bailey Park Elementary, Grinnell, Iowa.

Erika also was All-Conference and played on state-qualifying teams in basketball and softball. Harlan, one of Gretchen's brothers-in-law, and I were watching a game between Hudson and NESCO at the state softball tournament in Fort Dodge. NESCO was Harlan's home team, and he had been bragging about the pitcher for his team when Erika came to bat. She hit a home run and Harlan about fell off the bleachers. Erika rounded third, and her coach just stood in the box with her hands on her hips. She seemed strangely unhappy. Hudson won the game 2-1, so Erika's home run made the difference. The coach was unhappy because Erika had missed the bunt sign. Erika played both sports at Luther College and graduated with a degree in social work.

All of our children are married and have families of their own, leading successful, productive lives and making noteworthy contributions in their respective communities.

Horace Hegg designed his house in Hudson, Iowa, to fit a triangular-shaped lot that sloped from back to front.

New Generations

Prescott Hegg Arendt baptism, St. John's Lutheran Church
Grinnell, Iowa, August 2001

Erika Hegg-Arendt and Jack Arendt with children Philip and Prescott

Christian and Christine,
Caroline and Catherine Hegg

Sara Hegg-Dunne and Jim Dunne,
Eli, Nicole, and Katelin

Parents Philip and Kimberly Hegg with,
counterclockwise from top, Vincent, Zachary, and Sierra

The Horace and Gretchen Hegg
Family at the Millennium

b. 4/11/56   Philip Hegg
b. 9/19/59   Kimberly Smith Hegg   Zachary Taylor Smith
    b. 4/13/86
    Peter Vincent Smith
    b. 10/10/88
    Sierra Elise Smith
    b. 11/30/89

b. 6/19/59   Sara Hegg-Dunne
b. 11/02/58   Jim Dunne   Nicole Christine Dunne
    b. 2/10/84
    Katelin Marie Hegg Dunne
    b. 5/14/94
    Eli James Hegg Dunne
    b. 4/11/96

b. 11/13/62   Erika Hegg-Arendt
b. 6/07/61   Jack Arendt   Philip Hegg Arendt
    b. 7/15/97
    Prescott Hegg Arendt
    b. 6/16/01

b. 1/05/64   Christian Hegg
b. 5/29/68   Christine Taschler Hegg   Caroline Grace Hegg
    b. 3/23/98
    Catherine Ann Hegg
    b. 4/25/01

A New Era: Retirement Years

I had enjoyed the teaching experience and its everyday challenges. However, it was time to retire, and one is fortunate to know when that time arrives. I submitted my letter of resignation as a teacher in the Waterloo Schools as of June 5, 1993.

A year had passed, and I found the time to accept the position as building and financial chairman for the effort to build a new library in Hudson. Mabel Brown, wife of a prominent veterinarian and a former teacher in the Hudson schools, had donated fifty thousand dollars toward this goal. A large bond issue for a new high school had just passed, and the city government was thinking about redesigning the downtown streets and sidewalks. It was obvious that the money for a new library would have to come from private sources.

George Strayer had been president of the library board, and I had served on the board when the library moved from a few slide-out shelves in City Hall to a permanent spot in the basement. The old fire truck had found a new home, and the vacated space almost doubled the size of the library at that time. George was one of those who thought the school and the library should share a common ground, saving money on books, personnel, and utilities. That concept was not imminent in the late fifties in Hudson. He had passed away years before this new project was to unfold. I wonder what he would have thought about the ten thousand-square-foot library building that would be built right on the former site of the *Soybean Digest* building.

Mrs. George Strayer invited Gretchen and me to an evening dinner at the country club, where she was a member. We talked about the new plans for the building and the progress that had been made. We had raised another seventy thousand and would be asking for grants from some of the known philanthropies. Jeanne said she would consider a gift after she had gone over her finances.

I was dismayed to hear that she had passed away suddenly. I felt I had let the community down by not finding a way to let Jeanne participate in this worthwhile community project. Shortly before her death she had gone to her attorney. News soon came that she had specified in her will that one-third of her estate be preserved for the library-building project.

She had said to her attorney, "Now that is more than Mr. Hegg asked for." The amount was $466,000 and was the turning point in the campaign.

The library was built due to the best efforts of a number of people. It is ten thousand square feet and provides all the services one could anticipate from a first-class library, including an ICN site, which is networked across Iowa through the fiber-optic system. The eleven Internet computers are often in full use. Mary Bucy, the librarian, provided a beautiful grand piano through a family gift. Recitals are held during library hours, and anyone is free to play it at anytime.

The city government provided $150,000 as their part in the building project. One million seventy thousand was raised, and the new library after six years of struggle stands today, debt free, providing a variety of experiences for the young and old of Hudson and the adjoining rural population.

The new Hudson Public Library, July 1999
The library building committee included Horace Hegg, chairman,
Kathleen Holmes, Kristen Hargens, Jean Taylor Grinnell, Mary Bucy,
Joan Webster-Vore, Debbie Larsen, and Judy Shirley. Grant writers were
Charyl Einsweiler and Allen Ricks. Many volunteers also helped.

In the spring of 2002, it became apparent that Brinyild's Journey had to find a path leading to Norway. Vesterheim Norwegian-American Museum in Decorah, Iowa, the most complete representation of Norwegian culture in this hemisphere, was sponsoring a tour to Norway in celebration of its 125th anniversary. I said to Gretchen, "We're going to Norway with the tour."

It was July 30th when we drove the 100 miles from Hudson to Decorah. We joined Museum Director Janet Blohm Pultz and most of the tour group for the bus ride to Chicago, where we flew Scandinavian Airlines to Copenhagen, Denmark, and then a short flight to Oslo, Norway. The Grand Hotel, located in the heart of downtown Oslo, was our destination. This incredible city—with its impressive government and commercial buildings, its plaza with fountains, outdoor cafés, and statues of famous Norwegians—prompts visitors from the provinces and tourists from all over the world to mingle.

A formal dinner at the hotel that evening gave us a chance to get better acquainted with all the tour members. Movie star Arlene Dahl and her daughter were special guests. Ms. Dahl has had a long-standing interest in Vesterheim and she wanted to help celebrate the 125th anniversary dinner with us.

Arlene Dahl, actress, far right, daughter, center

Photographs of the tour to Norway are by Horace and Gretchen Hegg.

The Royal Palace

Sentry post at the king's palace, the guard at attention during his watch. His relief marched to the post in a stylized procedure known as the relieving of the guard, a traditional ceremony worldwide. One wonders if the sentry's weapon was armed and if he would have used it in the event of an unauthorized entry to the palace. Horace thinks one could walk up to this fellow and paint a moustache on his upper lip and the fellow wouldn't even blink.

The next morning, we took a tour bus to The Viking Ship Museum, then to the explorer Thor Heyerdahl Museum. We then visited the Vigeland Sculpture Park, where numerous sculptures depicting the ages of man are displayed. The next day, we went to a museum that told the story of the resistance movement to the German occupation during the Second World War. We completed the afternoon by touring the king's palace.

This sculpture on the grounds of the Viking Ship Museum in Oslo captures the essence of the ship with its high, gracefully curving bow that could lead the ship through the ocean waters. The bow was the distinguishing feature of the craft sailed by the Viking marauders who struck fear in the hearts of victims as far away as Rome. The museum features two Viking ships preserved from the Viking era as well as a highly decorated wooden wagon and a variety of tools from early medieval times.

The Vigeland Sculpture Park, Oslo

*Gustav Vigeland devoted his life to sculpting larger-than-life-size figures
in marble, bronze, and iron for the park. A 60-foot-long marble monolith
was brought by barge and erected at the north end of the park.
The sculptor died before the installation was complete.*

*Gretchen Hegg is in front of the Norwegian
parliament building in Oslo on a late summer evening.*

Early the next day, we boarded a jet for Kirkenes, where we'd board the eight-deck luxury cruise liner *M/S Finnmarken* for a four-day cruise down the coastal waters. This northern-most Norwegian city was the second-most-bombed city in Europe. The Russian Air Force made more than 325 bombing raids on the city to prevent the German army assembled there from launching a ground attack on the important Russian seaport of Murmansk. Of the 400 buildings in the city at the start of the war, only a few were left at war's end, and the Germans burned these as they evacuated the North Country. Russian aid of food and shelter helped survivors through the harsh winter that followed.

A 6,000-year-old petroglyph of reindeer and other wild animals carved in rock in the Valdres Valley. Petroglyphs are found in various sites in Norway and are evidence of early man's presence in Norway in the post-glacial age.

The M/S Finnmarken *is in a narrow fjord, inching along the side of a high rock cliff. A narrow opening in the wall allowed the captain to sail into the fjord. The tourists could almost reach out and touch the walls from either side. To get out, the captain slowly turned the ship in its own space and headed back to the coastal waters.*

But first, we traveled by tour bus 60 miles south along the Pasvik River to Skogfoss. Our guide, Pål Espolin Johnson, arranged for our group to be guests of his friend Odd Emanuelsen, his wife, Natanja, and grown children Karine and Aksel. We enjoyed a picnic at the campsite along the river close to Odd's modern home. A fresh catch of white fish was broiling on the grill. Karine prepared large bowls of lingonberries and cloudberries as a special treat with a variety of home-baked breads, cheeses, and potato salad, boiled potatoes, pies, and pastries. Aksel replenished a huge iron coffee pot with gallons of river water. The pot boiled merrily away over the campfire and the steaming hot coffee tasted better than most.

As we explored the campsite, we could see Russia less than a mile across the river. These are friendly times between the two countries, and employment may be found as though there was no boundary.

Odd was a farmer whose family emigrated to the North Country from southern Norway about the time many were emigrating to America; hence, this area of Norway is sometimes called "Little America."

Two accordion players played Norwegian folk music. Odd greeted us in his native language and we all understood his heartfelt message of welcome.

Later, we boarded the *M/S Finnmarken*, the newest of a fleet of eleven ships that sail from the seaport of Bergen to Kirkenes and back. We enjoyed the four-day cruise, which took us through the coastal waters in beautiful weather.

We visited the North Cape, a famous overlook of the Arctic Ocean.

We saw reindeer grazing near the roadway and visited a Saami campsite. The Saami of the North Country own reindeer herds and lead a nomadic life, moving from one grazing ground to another. Their colorful costumes and jewelry-making find a ready market in the tourist trade.

During the voyage, we left the ship for three separate bus tours to places of interest.

The Saami live in the north of Norway, Sweden, and Finland. Author Hegg is shown with a young Saami. This camp was near the North Cape of Norway, accessible for tour buses. Accepting credit cards, they offered handmade boots, mittens, vests, and headgear made from reindeer hides, along with handwoven woolen sweaters, a source of income in the summer season.

Another tour took us to the fishing villages of the Lofoten Islands. We took a third bus tour down the coast of a large fjord, requiring a ferry ride across the fjord to the road leading us back to the ship. This was one of the highlights of the tour for me. Three young Norwegian girls had set up a small stand to sell their artwork to passengers getting off the ferry. I asked if I might take their picture and then purchased a drawing from one of them.

I was startled to see that it was a caricature of a small boy who could have been Brinyild in my early years in Decorah, Iowa. Here was a Norwegian Brinyild created in the mind of this young girl.

Three young artists sell their work by a fjord near the ferry.

A side view of the majestic Nidaros Cathedral in Trondheim, where national ceremonial events and the coronation of kings are held.

We disembarked at Trondheim, the third-largest city in Norway and one of the oldest dating back to Viking times. As we settled in Trondheim, our guide, Pål, turned over his duties to a close associate. Birgit Jaastad, who is an equally renowned personage in Norway, led us through Trondheim, then to the ancient copper-mining town of Roros, then to the city of Fagerness in the lush Valdres Valley, and finally to Lillehammer, where she is a conservator at the Maihaugen Museum after which the Vesterheim Museum is modeled. Our two guides set the tone for our group with their ready sense of humor, their love of people, and their love for Norway.

The Stave Church at Maihaugen
This church was moved to this outdoor folk museum at
Lillehammer and rebuilt on its present site. The people
are attending a wedding.

Cousin Randi Hamre Berge, left, visits in her home with Gretchen Hegg. Randi had met Gretchen's sister Marcia when she visited Norway. She is as much a new friend as she is distant family. Vesterheim Norwegian-American Museum offers genealogy services to help find family roots.

We met a relative of Gretchen's at Fagerness. Randi Hamre Berge invited us to her home, a mile from the hotel. Her small home, carefully designed, included heirloom pieces from far into the family's distant past

We arrived at Lillehammer to the Mølle Hotel, which had been a mill that was renovated to become a quaint hotel and restaurant. Our room was two stories above the millrace, and the sound of rushing water below our window made sleep come quickly. This city hosted the 1994 Winter Olympic Games.

Street scene in Fagerness

After leaving Fagerness the following morning, we visited famed artist and rosemaler Sigmund Årseth, who received us as guests at his hillside studio and home. He had introduced the art of rosemaling at the Vesterheim Museum and had recently completed a mural in its new reception hall. He was well acquainted with several in our group, and there were hugs and laughter as he renewed the old friendships.

Top: Outdoor oven behind Sigmund Årseth's home
Below: Interior view of the Årseth home

Our group had the morning to shop along the pedestrian shopping avenue. An antique car rally of one hundred cars proceeded slowly along the avenue, adding a special festive air. A Norwegian jazz band held a strategic spot and kept up a barrage of tunes. We divided the afternoon between the Olympic Village and the Maihaugen Museum. The museum, the largest in Norway, depicted life from glacial times to the present day. More than one hundred buildings are part of the outdoor display.

Barn from Highlandville, Iowa, now at the Emigrant Museum near Lillehammer, Norway. Horace and Gretchen had visited Highlandville, ten miles from Decorah, Iowa, only a few months earlier. Imagine their surprise to find this barn built by Norwegians who came to America. It was dismantled and shipped to the museum. A small church in the background came from southern Minnesota.

Our tour ended that evening with a sit-down dinner of reindeer meat as the entrée. A toast was given and the wine flowed at the special banquet hall reconstructed on the museum grounds. On Sunday, August 11, we flew from Oslo to Copenhagen, then to Chicago, then rode a bus to Decorah, and finally, at 1 A.M. we drove home to Hudson. I reflected on one of the many things I wished to remember of our trip:

Foremost, the people of Norway: The shopkeepers, bus drivers, porters, ship's crew, guides, and hotel personnel were friendly, patient, of good humor, and handsome. One could see the Nordic genes in their faces and as outdoor people, they moved with the ease of hikers. The people are the riches of Norway.

As I reflect on my journey through life, a final thought:
Keep looking ahead of where one is playing the notes and forget about the
ones that might have been played a little better.

—*Horace Brinyild Hegg*